François de Salignac de La Mothe- Fénelon

Spiritual Letters of Archbishop Fénelon

Letters to Women

François de Salignac de La Mothe- Fénelon

Spiritual Letters of Archbishop Fénelon
Letters to Women

ISBN/EAN: 9783337016296

Printed in Europe, USA, Canada, Australia, Japan

Cover: Foto ©Lupo / pixelio.de

More available books at **www.hansebooks.com**

SPIRITUAL LETTERS

OF

ARCHBISHOP FÉNELON

LETTERS TO WOMEN

Translated

By the Author of "Fénelon, Archbishop of Cambrai"
"Bossuet and his Contemporaries"
"S. Francis de Sales," "Spiritual Letters of S. Francis de Sales"
etc. etc.

RIVINGTONS
WATERLOO PLACE, LONDON
Oxford and Cambridge
MDCCCLXXVII

CONTENTS.

LETTER		PAGE
I.	To the Duchesse de Beauvilliers. On Meditation and Prayer	1
II.	To the Comtesse de Gramont. On the Difficulties of a Worldly Life	15
III.	On a Scandal lately arisen	16
IV.	Simplicity in Action	19
V.	Need for Devotion amid a Worldly Life	20
VI.	Conduct in the World	24
VII.	Not to be troubled about Unintentional Omissions in Confession	27
VIII.	On Silence and Recollection	29
IX.	Avoiding Scruples	31
X.	Evils of a Disdainful Manner	33
XI.	Concerning Scruples about Common Things	34
XII.	Real Humanity	36
XIII.	How to meet Trial	39
XIV.	The same Subject	41
XV.	Prejudice	42
XVI.	Peace amid Trial	43
XVII.	Not to postpone Plans of Amendment	45
XVIII.	A Holy Life possible Everywhere	47
XIX.	Preparation for Advent	51

LETTER		PAGE
XX.	Advantages of a Humiliating Illness	53
XXI.	Rules for a Busy Life	54
XXII.	Support under Difficulty	55
XXIII.	Patience under God's Hand	56
XXIV.	On the Comte de Gramont's Recovery	58
XXV.	God's Crosses safer than Self-chosen Crosses	59
XXVI.	The Practice of Recollection at By-times	63
XXVII.	Faults to be met with a Vigorous Spirit	66
XXVIII.	Freedom from Self	67
XXIX.	To the Comtesse de Montberon (to Letter LXI.). A Simple Mind	70
XXX.	Some Rules as to Dress	71
XXXI.	On Meditation	73
XXXII.	On the Sickness of a Friend	75
XXXIII.	On the Death of the Same	77
XXXIV.	The Beginnings of Divine Love	78
XXXV.	Scruples	80
XXXVI.	The Source of Scruples	82
XXXVII.	Danger of Scruples	84
XXXVIII.	Love of God the Antidote to Scruples	86
XXXIX.	How the Love of God lightens Suffering	88
XL.	Care of Health and Duty	90
XLI.	Patience with Self	91
XLII.	Evil of Scruples	93
XLIII.	Forebodings to be avoided	94
XLIV.	How to accept Encouragement	96
XLV.	Discretion in Practice	97
XLVI.	Dangers of a Self-tormenting Spirit	98
XLVII.	Self-will in Religious Exercises	101

LETTER		PAGE
XLVIII.	God's Gifts to be welcomed from whatever Source	102
XLIX.	"I see another Law . . . warring against the Law of my Mind"	104
L.	Separated Friends meet in God	105
LI.	Perseverance	107
LII.	Not to foster Scruples	108
LIII.	Of some Social Perils	109
LIV.	Self-deceit	111
LV.	On the Privation of Sensible Sweetness . .	114
LVI.	The Struggles of Self-will	115
LVII.	The Cross Everywhere	117
LVIII.	A New Year's Wish	117
LIX.	On being kept back from a Sermon . . .	118
LX.	The Danger of Self-chosen Plans . . .	119
LXI.	To the Marquise de Risbourg. On Self-seeking in Friendship	120
LXII.	On Slackness in Religious Life	121
LXIII.	To a Lady (the same till No. LXX.). Hearkening to God	123
LXIV.	How to meet Sickness	124
LXV.	On giving way to the Imagination . . .	125
LXVI.	The same Subject	126
LXVII.	On Meditation	126
LXVIII.	The Value of Privations	127
LXIX.	How to use Eager Aspirations	128
LXX.	To a Lady living in the World. On her Desire for Knowledge	130
LXXI.	Dangers of Human Applause	131
LXXII.	How to bear Affronts	133

LETTER		PAGE
LXXIII.	Recollection in a Life of Restraint	135
LXXIV.	Patience under Contradiction	137
LXXV.	Benefits of looking Death in the Face	138
LXXVI.	The Necessity and Benefit of Suffering	139
LXXVII.	Need of calming Natural Activity	141
LXXVIII.	Forbearance to Others	142
LXXIX.	To One entering the Religious Life. On Calmness of Mind	143
LXXX.	All for God	145
LXXXI.	How to do all in the Spirit of Prayer	146
LXXXII.	Care of Health and Duty	148
LXXXIII.	Over-eagerness	149
LXXXIV.	Patience in Spiritual Privation	150
LXXXV.	In Sickness and Trial	152
LXXXVI.	Lukewarmness	154
LXXXVII.	How to bear with Others	155
LXXXVIII.	Impressions caused by the Prospect of Death	156
LXXXIX.	To a Religious in Illness	158
XC.	On Dryness in Devotion	159
XCI.	How to use Seasons of Spiritual Peace	162
XCII.	On the Prospect of Death in Old Age	163
XCIII.	On some Difficulties of Temperament	165
XCIV.	To a Lady recovering from Sickness	168
XCV.	Combined Exactitude and Freedom	170
XCVI.	To One in Retirement	174
XCVII.	Forbearance to Others, and to Self	175
XCVIII.	On seeking Help in Interior Trouble	177
XCIX.	On Openness and Candour	178
C.	Self-love	180

LETTER		PAGE
CI.	To a Lady. Concerning certain Family Difficulties	181
CII.	To a Lady who was Anxious concerning her Son	182
CIII.	God to be served in Ordinary Ways	184
CIV.	How to accept all God's Dealings thankfully	186
CV.	Self-consciousness	188
CVI.	Fearfulness	191
CVII.	To a Lady in Sickness	192
CVIII.	To the Same	194
CIX.	To One in Great Trouble	194
CX.	To One suffering from Jealousy	196
CXI.	The Restlessness of Self-conceit	197
CXII.	To a Lady. On the Death of her Husband	199
CXIII.	To the Duchesse de Chevreuse, some time after her Husband's Death	200
CXIV.	To the Young Duchesse de Montemart. On some Domestic Troubles	204
CXV.	To the Duchesse (Douairière) de Montemart. On bearing Reproof	206
CXVI.	To the Same. In Reply to some Questions concerning Self-knowledge	208
CXVII.	To the Same. On Crosses	213
CXVIII.	To La Sœur Charlotte de Saint-Cyprien. On the Dangers of Intellectual Attractions	214
CXIX.	To the Same. On the same Subject	215
CXX.	To the Same. Sickness a true Penitential Exercise	216
CXXI.	To La Mère Marie de L'Ascension, the Archbishop's Niece. On the Duties of a Superior	219

Contents

LETTER		PAGE
CXXII.	To One about to enter the Religious Life. On Indecision and Weakness	222
CXXIII.	To a Novice about to be professed	224
CXXIV.	To a Lady. On Confession and Communion	226
CXXV.	On the Employment of Time	231
CXXVI.	To One living in the World. On the Lawfulness of Amusements	235
CXXVII.	To a Lady at Court. The Burden of Prosperity	243
CXXVIII.	To a Lady at Court. God's various Crosses	247
CXXIX.	On Excessive Sensitiveness to Trials	252
CXXX.	God's Severity all Love	253
CXXXI.	Christian Perfection	256
CXXXII.	Simplicity and Self-consciousness	262
CXXXIII.	The Presence of God	275
CXXXIV.	On Conformity to the Will of God	279
CXXXV.	Inward Peace	284
CXXXVI.	On Gratitude	286
CXXXVII.	To One in Spiritual Distress	290
CXXXVIII.	The Life of Peace	293

LETTERS TO WOMEN

I.

TO THE DUCHESSE DE BEAUVILLIERS.
ON MEDITATION AND PRAYER.

I SEND what you ask for, Madame. . . . In order to make your prayer profitable, and as earnest as you desire, it would be well from the beginning to figure to yourself a poor, naked, miserable wretch, perishing of hunger, who knows but one man of whom he can ask or hope for succour; or a sick person covered with sores and ready to die, unless some pitiful physician will take him in hand and heal him. These are true representations of our condition before God. Your soul is more bare of heavenly treasure than that poor beggar is of earthly possessions; you need them more urgently, and there is none save God of whom you can ask or expect them. Again, your soul is infinitely more sin-sick than that sore-stricken patient, and God alone can heal you. Everything depends on His being moved by your prayers. He is able for all this; but remember that He wills only to do it when He is asked earnestly, and with real importunity.

When once penetrated with this truth, as you ought to be in order to set about prayer rightly, then proceed to read over the subject of your meditation, either in Holy Scripture or in whatever book you may be using. Pause after a verse or two, to follow out such reflections as God may put into your mind. And in order to help forward your beginnings, to rouse your mind from its ordinary inattention, and accustom it to fix upon the subject of meditation, you would do well to make an act of adoration of the Word, God's oracle, by which He teaches us His Will; of thankfulness, that He vouchsafes so to teach us; of humility, because hitherto you have not heeded His teaching better, or profited more by it, examining wherein you have specially neglected it, or are neglecting it, and how far your life has been in conformity or in opposition to it.

It is well, too, to think how Jesus Christ Himself practised the truth or the precept which He is teaching you; how those pious persons whom you yourself know are practising it; how the world neglects it; how you have departed from it, and why? Then lay your shame before God, literally prostrating yourself before Him in the solitude of your closet, and expressing by that outward posture the humiliation of your soul at the spectacle of your faults.

Then reflect upon the occasions which cause you to

commit these faults; the best means of avoiding or remedying them; what Jesus Christ justly requires of you, that you may keep from such falls and repair the past; how greatly you are bound to obey, however hard it may seem; how profitable it is to do so, how disgraceful and perilous to leave it undone. Remember that we are weakness itself, as daily experience proves, and offer yourself to Jesus Christ; abhor your cowardice and faithlessness; pray Him to fill your heart with all that He would see in it; ask Him to strengthen this will, so that you may go on doing better and better; trust in His Goodness, and in His solemn promises never to forsake us in time of need. Lean upon His Words, and rest in the hope that He will confirm that which He has wrought in you so far.

In order to make all this plain to you, Madame, I will give you an illustration of what I mean. Supposing the subject of your meditation to be the first words of the 17th chapter of S. John, which I was studying just before I began to write to you—Jesus Christ addressing His Father, and saying, "I have glorified Thee on the earth: I have finished the work which Thou gavest Me to do. And now, O Father, glorify Thou Me with Thine Own Self," etc.—I. Thank Jesus Christ for thus teaching you that you cannot aspire to the glory prepared for you by God save by glorifying Him upon earth. This is an unchangeable law, and one expressly taught by our Lord to all His followers in these words. The glory you have rendered to God on earth makes your claim to ask for that glory He has promised you in Heaven, and without it you have no right to aspire thereto.

II. Consider what is meant by glorifying God on the earth. Jesus Christ explains it clearly in the words, "I have finished the work which Thou gavest Me to do." So that to glorify God we must know and perform that which He gives us to do. Every one has his own work, and every one follows it out, but not always that work which God has given him to do. Our only work is that of Jesus Christ—namely, to work out our salvation, for which He worked during all His earthly sojourn. All the work which I undertake from vanity, from a desire to get on in the world, from temper, fancy, taste, self-will, or human respect, is not that which God has given me to do, and consequently none of this can glorify Him; all such is the work of the world, the flesh, or the devil.

III. The work God has given me to do is to amend whatever is amiss in my natural disposition—that is what He would have me do; correct my faults, sanctify my desires and longings, become more patient, more meek and lowly of heart. This, Madame, is your work; and to make the service of Jesus Christ prominent in your household, to bring up your family solely for Him, to train it in indifference to the world, in gentleness, patience, modesty, and a real love of God. Examine whether you are doing this, and how you are doing it.

IV. To avoid self-delusion, consider how Jesus Christ laboured all His Life at the work which His Father gave Him to do—unremittingly, never pausing for a moment—and draw your own example thence. If your God could devote His whole Life unbrokenly to you, what should not you do for Him? How ashamed you should be at having hitherto done so little—might one not wellnigh say nothing? Humble yourself deeply for this.

V. Consider what the Saints have done, and are still setting before you as an example. The work which God gave them to do was often much harder than that which He gives you. They had fewer means and helps towards accomplishing it than you have; they were as weak, and subject to as many difficulties and hindrances, yet they achieved their end. Acknowledge your own lack of energy in this matter; condemn your negligence. Thank God for the helps He has given you, ask His forgiveness for having used them hitherto so little and so badly, and offer yourself to Jesus Christ, asking His Grace henceforth to use them better.

VI. If we reflect upon all that we have done during our life, we may perhaps discover that it has all tended to ruin God's work, both in ourselves and in others, and to promote the work of sin and of the devil. When have we done that which God required of us, and how have we done it? When have we refused to follow the dictates of self-will and natural temper, and how much have we given way to them? How deep should be our regret and shame at seeing that we have done little or nothing to glorify God, but that our chief work has been dishonouring Him on earth! What a grief to have worked nearly all our life, and that, too, with satisfaction, against God and for the devil! Can we endure such a sight, or think upon a life so misused, without the deepest indignation against self, and sorrow before God?

VII. My God, has my occupation been to frustrate Thy work? Have I employed money, health, influence, intellect, authority, knowledge, position to Thy dishonour, and to the overthrow of that which Thou wateredst with Thine Own Blood? Have I found delight in that which cost Thee Thy Life? In spite of all Thy warnings, I have sold myself to Thy enemy, to promote his glory rather than Thine, without hope of reward, without prospect, save endless misery! Who could follow out such thoughts, Madame, without bitter grief? Neither reading nor argument is needed for one who realises all this duly. Let it sink into your heart, and cherish so wholesome a sorrow. Then go into further detail.

VIII. I speak and act on behalf of the devil whenever

I say or do that which is prompted by any evil temper; I set forward his work, and overthrow that of Jesus Christ within me, the work which He has begun by giving me a will and wish to do better. How, O my God, canst Thou bear with me, when I can scarce bear with myself? Dare I destroy within me the work which has cost Thee so dear in order to indulge my temper, or the passions which I know to be evil and unreasonable? Gentleness is Thy work, my God, and it is the work Thou hast given me to do. I cannot glorify Thee save by striving after and fulfilling it in myself. I will do so, my God; help me to persevere by Thy Mercy. Rather may all belonging to my home and family be upset than Thy work, and that by my own weakness!

IX. I will then give myself up to this one endeavour, since it is what Thou requirest of me. O God, am I called to put up with being badly served? I will do so gladly, if only I can thereby serve Thee well. My work is not to be well served, but to serve Thee well, to be gentle and patient under all that puts me out. In this way I can glorify Thee on earth; in this way only I can hope one day to be glorified of Thee in Heaven.

There are a thousand like matters in daily life, which I cannot enumerate here, but which you can see for yourself how to deal with, so as to seek in prayer for strength from God to amend what is amiss and confirm what is good. When you feel any of these things keenly, let God's Holy Spirit have full play in you, without interruption of reading or vocal prayer. But if your devout thoughts evaporate, and others come distracting you, humble yourself before God, and ask Him to fix your mind, and try to recollect yourself. If, nevertheless, such distractions return, then take your book, and go on to another point, making similar acts and reflections upon it.

At the end of your meditation, before leaving off, always ask God's forgiveness for your shortcomings, and be sure that even if you have been in a wellnigh continuous state of distraction, you will not have lost the time if you leave off more humble than before. Gather up whatever has touched you most, and go over it often during the day; that is the real way of "praying always." And if you can, renew the meditation more or less at night; it will help to stamp God's truths on your heart, and be very effectual. It will be well to begin your day with this. Take time for it before you dress, so as not to be hurried afterwards; but renew your meditation afterwards if you have time, and while dressing you can let your mind dwell upon what you have been meditating.

As to the very distracting occupations amid which you are of necessity placed, I must confess, Madame, that it would be desirable to be free from them. But as that is impossible, I would observe that whenever we have any trouble or care in our heads, we carry it everywhere about with us, and nothing can turn us aside from it; so if you are really sorry for your faults, and have a fixed resolution to please God and attain to salvation, nothing will be able to turn you from it. All your meditations should bear upon this.

The things which distract you the most are your duties with respect to the Queen, your father, and other relations. But indeed, Madame, all this may be of the greatest help to you in shaking off the distractions of which you complain. You did not seek office about her Majesty: you were called to it by God's Providence, and therefore it is a work committed to you by Him, and you must fulfil it in obedience to Him. The only thing to fear is lest you should lose sight of God and substitute vanity, pleasure, self-interest, or any merely earthly motives, and turn God's work into a sinful, selfish work. Your remedy is to reject all such if they molest you, abiding stedfastly in the performance of that which God has committed to you, and doing it as He would have it done.

What need hinder you, Madame, amid the worries of a household, from lifting up your heart to God continually, just as your people obey your orders, trying to please you as far as possible, bearing what vexes them in silence, delighted when you are satisfied? They only think and work for you, and you would not retain them long in your household if they forgot what is due to you, and thought only of themselves. And just what they all do for you in your house, you should do for God in your own position. Learn of your own domestics to be prompt in obeying His orders, in setting aside all that could offend Him, in correcting whatever may displease Him, in bearing such contradictions as He sends without complaint, in receiving correction humbly and gratefully, in thinking and toiling incessantly at the task He sets you; and so doing, the very things which ordinarily distract will promote your recollection, and lift your heart to God. And always remember, that just as you would not keep a servant who habitually neglected his work, or did it carelessly, so God will not tolerate a handmaid who does nothing, or does the work He sets her negligently or indifferently.

Everything which surrounds us in the world may tend to keep up our sense of the Presence of God. Truly the world has not much that is good, but somewhat there is, and that of itself leads us to thank God, and ask Him to strengthen those who do it, and lead us in the same paths. Evil abounds, and we continually come across it. But if you have any leaning to what is right, you will shrink from evil directly it encounters you, and there is not much fear lest it should take you by surprise. You dare not approve or commend it. There is more danger from certain evils which are less obviously abhorrent, and at which the world is wont to laugh and be entertained; and this, Madame, should be your real dread. Far from sharing any such noxious worldly amusement, you must grieve with all your heart that the children of God can find pleasure in that which caused our Dear Lord mortal grief. You must thank God for having called you forth from such a state, and fear lest He should leave you to fall back into the reprobate mind you see in others. Such thoughts as these will keep you from entering into the world's wickedness, or being contaminated by it. This is that "pure religion and undefiled" which S. James says "keeps itself unspotted from the world."

As to vocal prayers, of which you have none which are obligatory; say them slowly, striving to enter into the feelings excited by the words you repeat. Dwell upon their meaning, giving yourself time to do so thoroughly. Never be in a hurry to finish. Far better say half a Psalm well, than to run hastily through several. If any necessity interrupts, stop where you are, without being disturbed, and when you have leisure, begin again where you left off.

Never go to Holy Mass without thinking of the Sacrifice of Jesus Christ at which you are going to assist.

Try to obtain true contrition for your faults, which required that God should shed His Blood to cleanse them. Let your external modesty, and your devout attention to the holy ceremony, testify the spirit in which you approach it. I say nothing about the care you should take to restrain wandering glances, and whatever may distract your mind; this is the first thing to be done, and I am quite sure that you do it.

On the days that you go to confession, take your morning meditation time partly for self-examination, and the rest (which should always be the larger part) for asking due contrition and grace to amend. This is a good preparation. A still better is to keep more strict watch than usual over yourself for two or three days beforehand, performing some voluntary penance and good work while asking God for that sorrow for sin which you need. And when the week's record contains nought save sins of infirmity, I am not sure that it is necessary for you to confess them, or that it would not be better only to do as I have just said, for fear of making a mere habit of confession, and performing it sometimes without as much preparation as is to be desired. But this must depend upon the benefit you derive from more or less frequent confession, since that is what ought to regulate frequenting the Sacraments.

On the days when you communicate, you should pray

more than at other times. Remember that you do but receive Jesus offered in that Sacrifice to the end that you may offer and sacrifice yourself with Him, and live by His Life. He is full of life in the Sacrament, and He gives us life by it, but it is the life of a Victim. He feels the injuries done to Him therein, and bears them without displaying His Grief or His Power. This is the spirit of patience and of a Victim which you should receive if you communicate rightly. All your Communions must tend to this point. How much this requires of you!

Do not trust to your good intentions if they are barren and without result. Labour bravely to become gentle and humble of heart. If you commit any fault, and are able at once to withdraw to your closet, go and prostrate yourself on the ground before God, and ask forgiveness. Your sorrow and humiliation of heart will win you grace to be more faithful another time. Continually imitate our Lord's silence when He was maltreated by both judges and people. If something is done amiss which only affects you personally, and what is due to yourself, bear it silently. If any hasty word has escaped you, after inward humiliation for it, make amends by speaking kindly, and doing some little act of kindness, if possible, to those whom you have treated rudely. Never forget how God has dealt and does deal with you continually, how gently and patiently. Let that be your example;

learn from Him how to deal with others. Do not be disheartened by your falls. Inasmuch as they clearly point out your weak places, they ought to make you more humble, and more diligent in self-watchfulness and in constant recourse to God as a matter of preservation.

When you meditate, think that it is Jesus Christ Who is about to speak with you, and that concerning the most important of all concerns. Listen to Him accordingly. Read but little at once, and meditate much upon the truths you read. See how far and how earnestly you follow them. Ask Jesus Christ to speak to your inmost heart, and then to teach you what the book sets before you externally. If you find any severe condemnation of some one of your own faults, thank God for this merciful and unsparing rebuke, and pray Him yet further to correct you. Read Holy Scripture as much as you can, and such books as impress you most deeply. It is a good plan to mark the passages which strike you most, so as to repeat them at intervals during the day, and renew the feelings they kindled in you. When you have finished reading, always end with a short prayer, and ask God to enable you to practise what you have read when occasion offers.

II.

TO THE COMTESSE DE GRAMONT.
ON THE DIFFICULTIES OF A WORLDLY LIFE.

[Elizabeth Hamilton, daughter of the Marquis of Hamilton and Mary Butler, his wife. She was born in 1641, and married Philibert Comte de Gramont in 1660. This lady was a *dame-du-palais* to the Queen Marie Thérèse, and being of a devout mind, soon placed herself under Fénelon's direction. In 1692 the Comte de Gramont had a severe illness, to which reference is made in some of the following letters. His wife made use of the opportunities thus afforded for winning him to think of religion. In the *Journal de Dangeau* it is mentioned that the Comte was so ignorant of the very rudiments of devotion, that when his wife repeated the Lord's Prayer by his side, he exclaimed, "Comtesse, say that again; it is a beautiful prayer. Who made it?" After this time Fénelon's counsels seem to have been as valuable and as acceptable to her husband as to the Comtesse, and they both retained a staunch friendship for him through all the period of his disgrace at Court. Their correspondence was continued for many years. The following twenty-eight letters are all addressed to this lady.]

PARIS, *June* 11 (no year dated).

I WAS out of town, Madame, when you wrote to me

from your hermitage, or I should not have failed to obey your summons. . . . One thing is certain, namely, that I daily ask with all my heart that you may have all the recollection and faithfulness to God's Holy Spirit which you need to conquer the difficulties of your position. You have much to fear, both from within and from without. From without, the world smiles on you, and that side of the world which is most adapted to flatter your pride fosters it by all the consideration you are held in at Court. Then within, you have to conquer your taste for a refined life, your haughty, disdainful temperament, and a long-formed habit of dissipation. All this put together is a torrent likely to carry you away in spite of all your good resolutions. The real remedy for so many difficulties is to snatch, in spite of everything that hinders you, some fixed hours for prayer and reading. You know what I have more than once told you about this. I pray our Lord rather to take you from all, than to let you fall a prey to the world.

III.

ON A SCANDAL LATELY ARISEN.

Dec. 10, 1686.

I HEAR, Madame, that the scandal just burst forth has renewed the natural trouble which such affairs have caused you before. I sympathise exceedingly in all that grieves you. The thing I mind most in these unhappy events is that the world, always too ready to think evil of good people, assumes that there are none such on the earth. Some rejoice to think so, and triumph maliciously; others are troubled, and, in spite of a certain desire for what is good, they hold aloof from piety out of mistrust of the pious. People are astonished to see a man who has seemed to be religious, or who, more correctly speaking, has been really converted while living in solitude, relapse into old ways and habits on being once more confronted with the world. Did they not know before that men are frail, that the world is full of contagion, and that weak human beings can only stand upright by shunning occasions of falling? What new thing has happened? Surely this is a great fuss about the fall of a rootless tree, on which every wind blew! After all, are there not hypocrites in honesty as well as in religion to be found in the world? and ought we to conclude that there are no honest people because we find some false? When the world triumphs over a scandal like this, it shows how little it knows about mankind or about virtue. We may well be grieved at such a scandal, but those who know the depths of human frailty, and how even the little good we do is but as a borrowed thing, will be surprised at nothing. Let him who stands upright tremble lest he fall; let him who is prostrate, wallowing in the mire, not triumph because he sees one fall who seemed able to stand alone. Our confidence is neither in frail men nor in ourselves, as frail as others; it is in God only, the One Unchanging Truth. Let all mankind prove themselves to be mere men—that is to say, nought save falsehood and sin; let them be carried away by the torrent of iniquity, still God's Truth will not be weakened, and the world will but show itself as more hateful than ever in having corrupted those who were seeking after virtue.

As to hypocrites, time always unmasks them, and they are sure to expose themselves one way or another. They are hypocrites only with the object of enjoying the fruits of their hypocrisy. Either their life is sensual and pleasure-seeking, or their conduct self-interested and ambitious. One sees them cajoling, flattering, playing all manner of parts, whereas real virtue is simple, single-minded, free from *empressement* or mystery; it does not rise and fall, it is never jealous of the success or reputation of others. It does the smallest amount of wrong that it can, lets itself be criticised in silence, is content with small things, is free from cabals, manœuvres, pretensions. Take it or leave it, it is always the same. Hypocrisy may imitate all this, but very roughly. If it deceives any one, it will be only through their lack of perception or of experience in real virtue. People who do not understand diamonds, or who do not examine them closely, may take false stones to be real; but all the same there are such things as real diamonds, and it is not impossible to distinguish them. One thing is true, and that is, that in order to trust fair-seeming people, we should be able to recognise their conduct as simple, stedfast, solid, and well tried under difficulty, free from affectation, while firm and vigorous in all that is essential.

IV.

SIMPLICITY IN ACTION.

June 12, 1689.

I AM well, thank you, Madame, doing credit to quinine, and fit to silence its enemies. Your kindness gives me real pleasure, and I am grateful to my fever for inducing it. You go too far, Madame, in your discretion; if you want to see me, you have but to say so. A simple, straightforward line of action is too much after God's Own Heart ever to disturb those who wish to serve Him, and who are bound to speak in His Name, and teach simplicity. I hope you may be able to arrange the troublesome business which brings you to Paris. I fancy you will find a very drunken man in . . . ; the journey will have excited him. There are very various kinds of drunkenness. Holy Scripture speaks of those that "are drunken, but not with wine."[1] There is the drunkenness of pride, of anger, and of vengeance; and there is another kind altogether, of zeal and fervour. It was with this latter that the Apostles were filled when they received the Holy Ghost.[2] I shall hope to see you in this latter condition, Madame, when you return. And I shall still pray for you heartily.

V.

THE NEED OF DEVOTION IN A WORLDLY LIFE.

Oct. 2, 1689.

It seems to me, Madame, that you have two points to consider—one with respect to your engagements, the other with respect to yourself. The first consists in the care you should take to redeem some brief time from the world for reading and prayer. I can almost fancy I see all your difficulties, so thoroughly do I understand them. But after all, engagements must each have their own due weight, and what concerns salvation must certainly rank foremost. What would you think of a person who could not make time to eat and sleep? Surely you would tell him that the time given to that which is necessary to life is well spent, even as regards business itself. If health breaks down, what are you to do? and of what avail is

[1] Isa. xxix. 9. [2] Acts ii. 13.

all your work if you do not live to reap its fruits? It is just that I would say to you, Madame;—if you let your soul grow faint and exhausted for want of nourishment, of what avail is all the religious talk, or even the fulfilment of urgent and indispensable duties? Martha, Martha, you are eager and troubled about many things; but Mary, who sits by calm and recollected, has chosen the better part, which will never be taken from her. All the same, Madame, I do not speak thus in order to rouse scruples concerning your necessary occupations; but rest assured that necessary occupations will never extend so far as to deprive you of time to take your daily bread. God is too good, and He has made you too keenly alive to His Mercies, ever to deprive you of opportunities for prayer and for maintaining the pious feelings He has kindled in you. Try, then, to rescue half an hour morning and evening. If you claim half an hour's more rest in the one season, and retire half an hour earlier at night, as you might do to write some necessary letter, you would accomplish this, and none the less fulfil your real duties. You must learn, too, to make good use of chance moments: when waiting for some one, when going from place to place, or when in society where to be a good listener is all that is required;—at such times it is easy to lift the heart to God, and thereby gain fresh strength for further duties. The less time one has, the more carefully it should be husbanded. If you wait for free, convenient seasons in which to fulfil real duties, you run the risk of waiting for ever; especially in such a life as yours. No, make use of all chance moments. The claims of piety differ from those of temporal concerns. These latter require stated clear seasons which allow of a connected, continued application; but religion is not dependent upon such consecutive pursuit. One moment will suffice to place yourself in God's Presence, to love, and worship Him, to offer all you are doing or bearing, and to still all your heart's emotions at His Feet. So I intreat you, Madame, seize some half-hour at night and morning in which to repair the world's inroads, and during the day avail yourself of whatever considerations move you most, with a view to placing yourself in the Presence of God.

The other special point you have to heed is not to be disheartened, either by your conscious weakness, or by disgust at the life of excitement which you lead. It is God's Mercy which makes you grieve at this excitement, and that grief is the antidote which saves you from being corrupted by the dissipation of your Court life. So I should be very sorry if you ceased to feel that life irksome; I downright rejoice in your vexation and grief. God will teach you how to root out self through your disgust for worldly things, if it be sincere, amid the world itself; just as He teaches the same lesson to others in solitude, and by deprivation of all the world's attractions. The one thing is to be faithful, patient, and quiet under your actual crosses, which you have not chosen for yourself, but which God has allotted to you of His Own Good Pleasure. As to faults, they are harder to bear with; but they will turn to good, provided we use them to our own humiliation, without slackening in the effort to correct ourselves. Discouragement serves no possible purpose; it is simply the despair of wounded self-love. The real way of profiting by the humiliation of one's own faults is to face them in their true hideousness, without ceasing to hope in God, while hoping nothing from self. No one ever more urgently needed to be humbled by their faults than yourself; thus only will God crush your pride and confound your presumption. When He has stripped you of all self-resource, He will begin to build for Himself; till then He will overthrow every attempt by means of your own faults. Let Him work His Will; do you toil on humbly, without counting for anything.

VI.

CONDUCT IN THE WORLD.

Feb. 23, 1690.

I AM very glad, Madame, to hear that at last you have contrived to secure some solitary hours. Postponing the hour for seeing people as late as may be, and sometimes seeking shelter elsewhere—these are both good ways of defending yourself from importunate visitors. And at other times you may well cut short your intercourse with people whose only aim is amusement or unnecessary business. As to daily matters which appertain to your duties, or to providential arrangements, you can but put up with them patiently, however inconvenient or disturbing. It is a great consolation to remember that God is often hidden behind such disturbing conditions, as well as behind the most edifying friendships. Behind each importunate intruder learn to see God governing all, and training you in self-denial alike through a troublesome acquaintance as through the edifying examples of real friends. The former thwarts our will, upsets our plans, makes us crave more earnestly for silence and recollection, teaches us to sit loose to our own arrangements, our ease, our taste, our rest: he trains us to bend our will to that of others, to humble ourselves when impatience gets the better of us under such annoyance, and kindles a greater longing after God, even while He seems to be forsaking us because we are so disturbed.

I do not mean that we ought voluntarily to put ourselves in the way of dissipating influences: God forbid! That would be tempting God and seeking danger; but such disturbances as come in any way providentially, if met with due precaution and carefully guarded hours of prayer and reading, will turn to good. Whatever comes from God's Hand bears good fruit. Often those things which make you sigh after solitude are more profitable to your humiliation and self-denial than the most utter solitude itself would be. Let us be content to live day by day as God leads us, making good use of every moment, without looking beyond it. Sometimes an exciting book, a fervent meditation, or a striking conversation, may flatter your tastes and make you feel self-satisfied and complacent, fancying yourself far advanced towards perfection, and, by filling you with unreal notions, be all the while only swelling your pride, and making you come forth from your religious exercises less tolerant towards whatever crosses your will. I would have you hold fast to this simple rule: seek nothing dissipating, but bear quietly with whatever God sends without your seeking it, whether of dissipation or interruption. It is a great delusion to seek God afar off, in matters perhaps altogether unattainable, ignoring that He is beside us amid our daily annoyances so long as we bear humbly and bravely all those which arise from the manifold imperfections of our neighbours and ourselves.

I have but one word to say to you concerning love for your neighbour, namely, that nothing save humility can mould you to it; nothing but the consciousness of your own weakness can make you indulgent and pitiful to that of others. You will answer, "I quite understand that humility should produce forbearance towards others, but how am I first to acquire humility?" Two things combined will bring that about; you must never separate them. The first is contemplation of the deep gulf whence God's All-powerful Hand has drawn you out, and over which He ever holds you, so to say, suspended. The second is the Presence of that All-penetrating God. It is only in beholding and loving God that we can learn forgetfulness of self, measure duly the nothingness of that which has dazzled us, and accustom ourselves thankfully to "decrease"[1] beneath that Great Majesty which absorbs all things. Love God, and you will be humble; love God, and you will throw off the love of self; love God, and you will love all that He gives you to love for love of Him.

[1] John iii. 30.

VII.

NOT TO BE TROUBLED ABOUT UNINTENTIONAL OMISSIONS IN CONFESSION.

March 21, 1690.

I DO not think, Madame, that you need be anxious as to your past confessions and communions. If your beginnings were imperfect, at all events they were sincere, and your mistakes arose from a thing which is very contrary to your natural character—I mean simple obedience. Besides, it is well to remember that the validity of past confessions consists, not in having omitted no fault, but in having accused yourself honestly of all faults of which you were at that time conscious. At that time you had not the light which has been developing since to show you thoroughly many mainsprings of an evil, corrupt nature within you. As that light increases, we see ourselves to be worse than we thought. We are amazed at our former blindness as we see issuing forth from the depths of our heart a whole swarm of shameful feelings, like filthy reptiles crawling from a hidden cave. We never could have believed that we had harboured such things, and we stand aghast as we watch them gradually appear. But we must neither be amazed nor disheartened. We are not worse than we were; on the contrary, we are better. But while our faults diminish, the light by which we see them waxes brighter, and we are filled with horror. Bear in mind, for your comfort, that we only perceive our malady when the cure begins. So long as there is no sign of cure, we are unconscious of the depth of our disease; we are in a state of blind presumption and hardness, the prey of self-delusion. While we go with the stream, we are unconscious of its rapid course; but when we begin to stem it ever so little, it makes itself felt.

If you find that you have omitted definite matters of importance in former confessions, tell them plainly the next time you go to confession. Your Confessor is an upright, discreet, God-fearing man; as to all else, be at peace. Be sure that humility, frequent silence and recollection, will do you more good than any amount of anxiety and self-chosen austerities. Silence is, above all, important for you. Even when you cannot retire from the world, you might often practise silence, and let others take the lead in conversation. There is no way by which you can so effectually subdue your haughty, disdainful, contemptuous spirit, as by bridling it with silence. Keep a strict watch upon your tongue. The Presence of God, which restrains your words, will likewise keep all your thoughts and wishes in check. But this work must be accomplished gradually. Be patient with yourself, as well as with others.

VIII.

ON SILENCE AND RECOLLECTION.

I THINK, Madame, that you should try hard to learn to practise silence, so far as general courtesy will admit of. Silence promotes the Presence of God, avoids many harsh or proud words, and suppresses many dangers in the way of ridiculing or rashly judging our neighbours. Silence humbles the mind, and detaches it from the world; it would create a kind of solitude in the heart like that you court; it would supply much that you need under present difficulties. If you retrenched all useless talk, you would have many available moments even amid the inevitable claims of society. You wish for freedom for prayer; while God, Who knows what you need better than you do, surrounds you with restraints and hampering claims. The hindrances which beset you in the order of God's Providence will profit you more than any possible self-delectation in devotion. You know very well that retirement is not essential to the love of God. When He gives you time, you must take it and use it; but meanwhile abide patiently, satisfied that whatever He allots you is best. Lift up your heart to Him continually, without making any outward sign; only talk when it is necessary, and bear quietly with what crosses you. As you grow in the faith, God will treat you accordingly. You stand more in need of mortification than of light. The only thing I dread for you is dissipation; but you may remedy even that by silence. If you are stedfast in keeping silence when it is not necessary to speak, God will preserve you from evil when it is right for you to talk.

If you are unable to secure much time to yourself, be all the more careful about stray moments. Even a few minutes gleaned faithfully amid engagements will be more profitable in God's Sight than whole hours given up to Him at freer seasons. Moreover, many brief spaces of time through the day will amount to something considerable at last. Possibly you yourself may find the advantage of such frequent recollection in God's Presence more than in a regular definite period allotted to devotion.

Your lot, Madame, is to love, to be silent, and to sacrifice your inclinations, in order to fulfil the Will of God by moulding yourself to that of others. Happy indeed you are thus to bear a cross laid on you by God's Own Hands in the order of His Providence. The penitential work we choose, or even accept at the hands of others, does not so stifle self-love as that which God assigns us from day to day. In it we find nothing to foster self, and, coming as it does directly from His

Merciful Providence, it brings with it grace sufficient for all our needs. All we have to do is to give ourselves up to God day by day, without looking further; He will carry us in His Arms as a loving mother carries her child. Let us believe, hope, love, with a child's simplicity, in every need looking with affection and trust to our Heavenly Father. He has said in His Own Word, " Can a woman forget her sucking child? . . . Yea, she may forget, yet will I not forget thee."[1]

IX.

AVOIDING SCRUPLES.

May 28, 1690.

You are afraid lest you be unfaithful in your duties toward God, and you are right. Nothing is farther from grace than a cowardly soul, who, out of a spirit of independence, refuses or delays to do what God requires. But, at the same time, you must beware of scruples. Try to examine honestly what real courtesy demands. For instance, if, just at the moment you have allotted to devotional exercises, some one calls upon you who does not usually come at that hour, who has real business with you, with whom you are not sufficiently intimate to ask him or her to come at some other time, and who might

[1] Isa. xlix. 15.

reasonably be offended if you did so—then, Madame, you need have no doubt as to the propriety of leaving your devotions to comply with such a demand; but in such a case you should endeavour to make up the lost time at some other part of the day, as you would take a meal which had been inevitably deferred at a later hour. As for those people who have no real business in hand, or who can be postponed without inconvenience, or who only come for amusement' sake, I should be pitiless in sending them away if they come during your reserved hours.

No one ever needed inward nourishment, silence, reflection, separation from the world, mistrust of self and inclination, more than you. You cannot practise too rigid a fast from the charms of worldly talk. You must be continually lowering yourself—only too safe, as you are, to rise again overmuch. You must be lowly, become as a little child, seeking only swaddling-clothes and pap, and even then you will be a naughty child! All the crosses God sends you in order to bend your back have not yet conquered your pride. It will only be by dint of yielding in silence before God that you will become softened by grace. Talk when you are alone; you cannot talk too much then, for it will be to God that you will tell your weakness, your wants, and your longings. But in society you can scarcely talk too little.

Not that I want you to keep a cold, disdainful silence, but rather a silence full of deference to others. I should be delighted when you spoke only to praise, approve, sympathise, and edify; only I am sure that if this is all you do, you will find conversation very tame, and say but little! Restrain yourself within few and simple words, give the precedence to all other speakers, and try to be recollected even in conversation. You need this antidote more than most people.

X.

EVILS OF A DISDAINFUL MANNER.

June 22.

... I QUITE understand how you are both suffering yourself and causing others to suffer. You must work bravely and persistently in bearing the burden if you would relieve your neighbours. Everything like a proud or disdainful manner, all that savours of ridicule or censoriousness, indicates a self-satisfied mind, unconscious of its own foibles, a prey to fastidiousness, and finding pleasure in the troubles of others. There is nothing more humbling than this sort of pride; so easily wounded, disdainful, contemptuous, haughty, jealous of its own rights, implacable towards others. It is a proof that one is very imperfect indeed when one is so impatient with the imperfections of others. I see no remedy for all this save hoping in God, Who is as Good and Powerful as you are weak and bad. Yet probably He will let you grovel on for long without uprooting your natural disposition and long-formed habits; and that because it is far better for you to be crushed by your own frailty, and by the proof of your incapacity to escape from it, than to enjoy a sudden advance towards perfection. Only strive to bear with others, and to turn your eyes away from people who cannot edify you, as you would shut them to a temptation. They really are a very dangerous temptation to you. Pray, read, humble yourself by cultivating lowly things. Soften your heart by uniting it to the Child Jesus in His Patience and Humiliation. Seek strength in silence. . .

XI.

CONCERNING SCRUPLES ABOUT COMMON THINGS.

June 27, 1690.

I AM truly sorry for the distress you are in, and I think I see the cause plainly. If I could induce you to use the simple remedy I am about to suggest, you would soon be relieved; but I am afraid some scruple may hinder you.

Your spiritual progress is more hindered by your

excessive fear of giving way to enjoyment in ordinary, innocent things, than it could ever be by that enjoyment itself. Of course, self-indulgence is always to be avoided, especially when we need self-restraint; but you are seriously injuring yourself by keeping up a perpetual effort to resist even the smallest involuntary pleasure in the details of a well-regulated life. I would have you steadily repress all excessive fastidiousness and delicacy whenever you really perceive such tendencies; but I do not approve of your constrained efforts perpetually to reject the enjoyment inevitably attending upon simple food and needful rest. Since you are ordered to take milk, you ought to obey your doctor as regards fasting. After having stated your case plainly, you should submit without arguing; otherwise you will involve yourself endlessly, and fret yourself to no avail. Speak honestly to your doctor about whatever concerns your health, without seeking to be indulged; then leave him to decide, and give no heed to your own fancies. But obey quietly; that should be the aim of your courage and stedfastness. Without this you will not acquire the peace which God's children possess, nor will you deserve it. Bear all the annoyances of your present condition, which is full of inconveniences and discomfort, in a penitential spirit; these are the penances God assigns you, and far more useful than what you may choose for yourself. There is no spot in the world where you would not find yourself beset with your natural taste for enjoyment. Even the strictest solitude would have its thorns. The best state to be in is that in which God's Hand holds you; do not look beyond it, and be content to accept His Will from one moment to another in the spirit of mortification and self-renunciation. But this acquiescence must be full of trust in God, Who loves you all the more for not sparing you.

Take as much sleep as the doctor considers right with respect to your constitution and your present indisposition. You ought to be scrupulous about your scruples, rather than about your sleep!

XII.

REAL HUMILITY.

July 22, 1690.

THAT is false humility which believes itself unworthy of God's Goodness, and dares not look to it with trust. True humility lies in seeing one's own unworthiness, and giving one's self up to God, never doubting that He can work out the greatest results for and in us. If God's success depended on finding our foundations ready laid, we might well fear that our sins had destroyed all chance for us, and that we were unworthy to be accepted by His

Divine Wisdom. But God needs nothing that is in us; He can never find aught there save that with which He has Himself filled us. Nay, we may go further, and say that the absolute nothingness of the creature, bound up as it is with sin in a faithless soul, is the fittest of all subjects for the reception of His Grace. He delights to pour it out on such, for these sinful souls which have never experienced anything save weakness cannot claim any of God's gifts as their own possession. It is thus that, as S. Paul says, God chooses "the foolish things of the world to confound the wise." [1]

Do not fear then, Madame, that your past faithlessness need make you unworthy of God's Mercy. Nothing is so worthy thereof as utter weakness. He came from Heaven to earth to seek sinners, not just men; to seek that which was lost—as indeed all were lost but for Him. The physician seeks the sick, not the healthy. Oh, how God loves those who come boldly to Him in their foul, ragged garments, and ask, as of a Father, for some garment worthy of Him! You wait to be familiar till God shows a smiling Face; but I tell you that if you will open your heart thoroughly to Him, you will cease to trouble about the aspect of His Face. Let Him turn a severe and displeased Countenance upon you as much as He will; He never loves more than when He threatens, for

[1] 1 Cor. i. 27.

He threatens only to prove, to humble, to detach souls. Do you want the consolation which God can give, or God Himself? If it is the first, then you do not love God for His Own Sake, but for yours; and in this case you deserve nothing at His Hands. But if, on the contrary, you seek Him simply, you will find Him even more truly when He tries than when He comforts you. In the latter case you have cause to fear lest you should cleave more to His sweetnesses than to Himself; but when He deals roughly with you, and you hold on fast, it is to Him alone that you cling. Alas, Madame, how we deceive ourselves! We revel in delight when a conscious sweetness upholds us—we fancy ourselves in a seventh Heaven, and are lost in unreality; but if our faith is dry and cold, we grow disheartened, and think that all is lost, whereas in truth that is the real time for progress if we do not yield to discouragement. Leave it all to God; it is not your business to judge how He should deal with you, He knows far better what is good for you. You deserve a certain amount of trial and dryness; bear it patiently. God does His part when He repulses you; try to do yours too, and that is to love Him without waiting for Him to testify His Love for you. Your love is a guarantee of His; your confidence will disarm Him, and turn all His severity into tenderness. Even if He were not to grow tender, you ought to give yourself up to His just dealings, and accept His intention of nailing you to the Cross in union with the desolation of Jesus, His Beloved Son.

Such, Madame, is the solid food of pure faith and generous love with which you should sustain your soul. I pray that God may make you strong and vigorous under your troubles. Expect all, and all will be given you: God and His Peace will be with you.

XIII.

HOW TO MEET TRIAL

November 17, 1690.

I AM very sincerely grieved at your brothers' misfortunes,[1] but if they are forsaken of men, you must all the more win God's Help for them by your patience. He is the Shelter of all who are persecuted, and the Comforter of the afflicted. He is trying you through these events affecting your brothers; but He tries you only in order to your greater detachment, and that you may become more worthy of Him. "He that loveth father or mother or brother, or aught else, more than Me, is not worthy of Me."[2] You must sacrifice your own flesh and blood—

---

[1] Political troubles in England following upon the Battle of the Boyne.
[2] Matt. x. 37.

you must sacrifice yourself, to Him. He is our best Friend, and our closest Relative.

Also, Madame, what could you expect of men? Did you not know what they are? weak, blind, inconstant; some not willing to do what they can, others unable to do what they would. Man is but a broken reed; if one seeks to lean on it, the reed bends, and pierces one's hand. Practically, what I think is this: God has touched you to the quick in this humiliation; the Loving Physician has applied this remedy to a diseased, quivering surface. So much the better, He means to heal you. Be silent, adore the Hand which strikes; do not open your lips, save to say, " I have deserved it." Whatever you may say against the King and Queen will be in mere revenge, and cannot serve you. You would injure them without helping yourself. You cannot conscientiously say a word; such want of self-control would be scandalous. For my part, I think God was waiting for this opportunity, and that it will decide your spiritual progress. If you lose the fruits of such a cross, you will be doubly unfortunate, and you will fall most dangerously short of God's claim upon you. But what grace will come from it if you bear it bravely! It will be the entrance into a fresh path towards evangelic perfection. Do not hesitate, then; however bitter the cup may be, drain it to the dregs, like our Lord Jesus Christ. I pray Him to give you strength, and not to suffer you to give way to any unjust ebullitions of resentment. He died for those who slew Him, and He has taught us to love, bless, and succour with our prayers those who curse and persecute us. Redouble your prayers during this time of trouble and temptation. You will find all that is lacking to your heart, in order to love those whom your pride would fain hate and crush, in the Heart of Jesus, dying on the Cross.

XIV.

ON THE SAME SUBJECT.

Nov. 19, 1690.

You may rightly express your sorrow and grief at the misfortunes which have come upon your brother, and you may also show your great eagerness to help him by all innocent means; but you must beware of exhibiting resentment towards those who oppose him. It would only embitter him, and foster that spirit of hatred and revenge which you should strive to soothe. Do not tell him more than the precise facts which are necessary to his affairs, and important to a right understanding of his interests. Do not tell him details which can only tend to embitter his mind. In this way you will not only spare him temptation, but a great deal of mental pain.

XV.

PREJUDICE.

June 17, 1691.

You are continually called upon to suffer, both through yourself and in others. If you suffered only through others, and never yourself felt the evils you complain of in others, your unhappy neighbours would seem monsters only fit to be strangled! But God permits you to suffer from your own proud, unjust, rebellious spirit, in order to teach you to bear with what is irritating in other faulty people. I would have you observe that self-love is insatiable, and always ready to murmur. A few months ago you would have been only too thankful to have been certain of your brother's freedom, and of the pleasure of seeing him for two days before he returned to serve his King. All this has come to pass, and so far from thanking God for such unhoped-for mercy, you grumble because you have seen so little of him. Have a care lest you should see more of him than you would desire.

Why should you be so bitter against the King and Queen of England? Perhaps there are secret causes which make it impossible for them to do what you want; perhaps you are too exacting; perhaps they are prejudiced, and see things from a point of view different to yours. What then? do you consider prejudice an unpardonable crime? Is it not a weakness common to man? And who is altogether free from it, however well-intentioned? Have you never been prejudiced? Cannot you forgive the prejudices of others? Recall yourself, I beseech you, to common humanity, until such time as charity may soften your heart. If you cannot altogether restrain and moderate yourself, at least humble and check your pride, without admitting discouragement. Try to soothe yourself silently before God, as a mother soothes the child which is sobbing on her knees. By degrees calm will follow upon recollection. If only you will profit by your leisure at Dinan, and be diligent in prayer and reading, all will do well. Crosses are essential to you, and God, Who loves you, does not spare them. I pray that He will further give you strength to bear them.

XVI.

PEACE AMID TRIAL.

June 23, 1691.

I CANNOT be as sympathetic with your sorrow, Madame, as I fain would be; but I see so many tokens of mercy, and so abundant a harvest of grace for you therein, that if nature groans under it, faith must needs rejoice. You give up hope, but without hope you will find peace in submission and in unreserved sacrifice. This is just what God would have. He drives you to that, in order to detach you from whatever is not Himself. What is left for you but to grasp the Cross He sets before you, and let yourself be crucified? When that is fairly done, He will comfort you. But He does not give poisoned comfort, which only fosters the venom of self-love, as men do; He does not comfort until He has deprived our proud, self-seeking nature of every resource. The peace which you find in submission, without any change in outward matters, is a great gift. By it God trains you to bear trial without despondency; although your shrinking, weak nature is depressed, your inner mind is upheld. Such a peace is all the purer that it is somewhat bitter. Your daily bread just now is the thought of God, Whose right over you His creature is boundless; and that of your own weakness, which deserves nought save humiliation and crosses. You accept it all, but you cannot understand why God should purify the guilty by punishing the innocent. But remember, Madame, that no one is innocent, or fit to come before His Judgment. How do you know but that the same blow which humbles you will bend your brother likewise beneath God's Hand? We must adore His dealings, without seeking to fathom them. It may be that by so many trials He is drawing your brother to turn finally to Himself; perhaps the day will come when you will both rejoice over what now so greatly troubles you. Leave it all to God, man can do nothing. When all seems lost, all is sometimes most nearly saved. God casts us down, and brings us up from the precipice with His Own Hand. But whatever He may do for your brother, your part is to accept the Cross, and adore the Hand Which lays it on you. Happy they who are ready to accept everything; who never say, It is too much; who reckon, not upon themselves, but upon the Almighty; who ask only such measure of consolation as God wills to give them, and who live by His Will alone.

XVII.

NOT TO POSTPONE PLANS OF AMENDMENT.

Sept. 17, 1691.

I AM very glad, Madame, to hear that your health is restored. The mind you indicate proves that no cross is fruitless when accepted in the spirit of sacrifice. I hope that we shall see you return to Fontainebleau with renewed grace and detachment from the world. You are quite right in believing that it is no good to wait for freedom and retirement to overcome the old Adam and learn detachment. Such freedom is a mere fanciful idea.

perhaps never to be attained; and we ought to be prepared to live and die in the bondage of our calling, if Providence sees fit to thwart our plans for retiring. You are not your own mistress, and God only requires that of you which is in your own power. The Israelites when in Babylon yearned after Jerusalem; but how many of them never saw Jerusalem again, ending their days in Babylon! Supposing they had gone on delaying their faithful service of God and their efforts after holiness until they should be restored to their country, how great a delusion it would have been! Perhaps yours is a somewhat similar position.

I am touched at what you tell me of Mme. de la Sablière. I never saw her save once, when she struck me greatly. She is quite right to seek nothing from man since she has found God, but to sacrifice even her dearest friends to Him. The best Friend is within our heart, the Jealous Bridegroom, Who repulses all else. As to death, only worldly, carnal people dread it. "Perfect love casteth out fear." We cannot cast out fear by thinking highly of ourselves, but by loving with a single heart, and giving up ourselves unreservedly to Him we love. This renders death easy and welcome. To him who is dead to self bodily death becomes merely the consummation of the work of grace.

XVIII.

A HOLY LIFE POSSIBLE EVERYWHERE.

I CAN hardly recall, Madame, all that I said last Sunday. My general impression is that I told you two things: first, that we are bound to seek our sanctification in that state wherein Providence has placed us, rather than to build castles in the air concerning great possible virtue in positions we do not fill; and secondly, that we need very diligent faithfulness to God in the smallest things.

Most people spend the best part of their life in avowing and regretting their habits, in talking about changing them; in making rules for a future time which they look for, but which is not given them; and in thereby losing time which ought to be spent in good works and in setting forward their salvation.

You should treat all such notions as very dangerous. Our salvation ought to be the work of every day and every hour. No time is fitter for it than that which God in His Mercy accords us now; and that because to-day is ours, but we know not what to-morrow may bring forth. Salvation is not to be achieved by wishing for it, but by seeking it heartily. The uncertainty of life ought to make us realise that we should prosecute this undertaking with all our energies, and that all other pursuits are worthless, since they do not bring us nearer to God, the rightful End of all we do—the God of our salvation, as David continually calls Him in the Psalms.

Why do we make plans for advancing in perfection? Because we believe it necessary to our salvation. Why, then, do we defer carrying them out, when it is just as necessary to seek now after salvation as it will be ten years hence; now at Court, as hereafter in a more retired life? Surely it is wise always to take the safest side in whatever concerns salvation, a matter in which we lose all or gain all. That state of life to which God has called us is safe for us so long as we fulfil all our duties therein. If God foresaw that it was impossible to be saved at Court, He would have forbidden us to live in it. But so far from this, He has appointed Kings and their Courts, and gives men that birth and position which admits them to those Courts. So we may be sure that it is His Will that souls at Court should be saved, and find the narrow way to Heaven, the way of truth, that way which Jesus Christ has said "shall make us free"[1]—in other words, shall guide us out of all the dangers to which the world exposes us.

And so much the more you meet with these dangers in your present state of life, so much the more you must keep watch over yourself, that you yield not to them.

[1] John viii. 32.

Keeping watch over self means hearkening to God; it means always abiding in His Presence, being always recollected, never plunging into voluntary dissipation or distraction amid the things of this world; it means as far as possible caring for retirement, prayer, and good books; it means what David calls "pouring out your heart before God,"[1] feeling Him within you, seeking Him earnestly, loving Him above all else, avoiding whatever is displeasing to Him. Such goodness as this, Madame, is suitable to every state of life; it will be most helpful to any one living at Court, and I know nothing better adapted to teach you to be in the world without being of the world. Pray adopt it, and strive never to forget that you are with God and He with you, so that you may abide stedfast in His service.

Make a habit of frequently adoring His Holy Will by humbly submitting yourself to the order of His Good Providence. Ask Him to uphold you, lest you fall. Intreat Him to perfect His work in you, so that, having inspired you in your present state of life with the desire to be saved, you may actually work out your salvation therein. He does not require great things for success. Our Lord Himself has said, "The Kingdom of God is within you;"[2] we can find it there when we will. Let us do what we know He requires of us, and so soon as we

---

[1] Ps. lxii. 8.   [2] Luke xvii. 21.

perceive His Will in anything, let there be no drawing back, only absolute faithfulness. Such faithfulness ought not merely to lead us to do great things for His service and for our salvation, but whatever our hand finds to do, or which appertains to our state of life. If one could only be saved by means of great deeds but few could hope for salvation. It depends, however, in fulfilling God's Will. The smallest things become great when God requires them of us. They are only small as regards themselves; but they forthwith become great when done for Him, when they lead to Him, and serve to unite with Him eternally.

Remember how He has said, "He that is faithful in that which is least is faithful also in much, and he that is unjust in the least is unjust also in much."[1] I should say that a soul which sincerely longs after God never considers whether a thing be small or great; it is enough to know that He for Whom it is done is infinitely great, that it is His due to have all creation solely devoted to His Glory, which can only be by fulfilling His Will.

As to you, Madame, I think you should accept your crosses as your chief acts of penitence; the worries of the world ought to teach you to sit loose to it, and your weakness wean you from yourself. If you bear this continual burthen patiently, you cannot fail to advance in

[1] Luke xvi. 10.

the narrow way. It is narrow by reason of the sorrows which wring your heart; but it is broad by reason of the enlargement God vouchsafes to that heart. One may suffer, be surrounded by contrarieties—one may even be deprived of spiritual consolations, yet be free because one accepts all suffering without seeking deliverance. One bears one's own weakness, preferring it to more agreeable conditions, because it is God's choice. The great thing is to suffer without losing courage.

XIX.

PREPARATION FOR ADVENT.

THE season of Advent should kindle in us an earnest desire to give ourselves to God, to prepare our heart to receive the fulness of His Grace, and make ready to be born again with Jesus Christ—or, more correctly, to profit by His Birth through the union with Him which we need, and which only God's Love can create.

We ought each severally to hear as spoken to ourselves S. John's exhortation to the Jews, "Prepare ye the way of the Lord, make His paths straight,"[1] so that He may find us ready to receive Him and His Blessings. This preparation consists of an ardent desire to possess Him. For this reason the Church reminds us at this season of

[1] Matt. iii. 3.

the holy patriarchs' longing for the Coming of Messiah, Who is called the Desired of all Nations in Holy Scripture. We kindle this longing in prayer when we pour forth our hearts before God, and intreat Him to "raise up His Power and come among us." Our Lord Himself put this prayer into our mouth when He bade us ask, "Thy Kingdom come;" in other words, that He may reign within us, and we be bound by bonds of love to His Law and His Gospel.

Such longings are best nurtured in solitude; therefore, Madame, I counsel you to retire as often and as much as you can to seek God's Grace, believing that as He spake to S. John Baptist in the desert, and made known the Messiah to His people in the wilderness, so He will enlighten you and fill you with His Spirit, above all when you are trying to seek Him in retirement, and seeking to unite yourself to His Merits.

I would advise, then, that you spend much time in prayer, and that you take as subject-matter for your meditations the third chapter of S. Matthew, part of the first chapter of S. Mark, the third of S. Luke, and the first of S. John. There you will find the subject of S. John Baptist's exhortations to the people, which embody all we ought to do in preparation for the Coming of Jesus Christ into the world and into our hearts. His teaching may be summed up as follows:—

I. Repentance, leading us to separate from the world, to bemoan our past attachment to it, and to embrace the Gospel maxims as to the narrow way.

II. Humility, owning ourselves unworthy to appear before Jesus Christ, much more to be united with Him and to receive Him in our heart.

III. Real courage and firmness in what is right, never being discouraged by the difficulties which beset us, and vigorously resisting the world's stream.

XX.

ADVANTAGES OF A HUMILIATING ILLNESS.

Dec. 22, 1691.

YOUR letter has given me great pleasure, telling me that you are better, that you will return shortly, and, best of all, that you have tried to make good use of your trials. Whatever attacks your fastidiousness and proud sensitiveness will go straight to the mark. God knows how to choose just what we want, and the blows He deals are mercies. Your malady is more precious than all the natural gifts which bound you to the world. You are happy in having this penance laid on you; it should teach you to despise nothing, entertain horror for nothing, not to esteem yourself above any, and to bear with the infirmities of all. The leprosy of pride, self-love, and all such moral passions, would, but for our blindness, seem to us far more horrible and infectious than the most loathsome maladies which only affect the body. I await your return with sincere pleasure.

XXI.

RULES FOR A BUSY LIFE.

March 21, 1692.

INDEED, Madame, it is not I that am hard to find, it is you! Please to remember this, and don't talk any more about people keeping me like a relic! I dare not disturb you when surrounded by M. de Gramont, and so many others! Seriously, though I am sorry for your difficulties, you greatly need certain free hours to be given to recollection. Try to steal some such, and be sure that such little parings of time will be your best treasures. Above all, try to save your mornings; defend them like a besieged city! make vigorous sallies upon all intruders, clear out the trenches, and then shut yourself up within your keep! Even the afternoon is too long a period to let go by without taking breath.

Recollection is the only cure for your haughtiness, the sharpness of your contemptuous criticism, the sallies of your imagination, your impatience with inferiors, your love of pleasure, and all your other faults. It is an excellent remedy, but it needs frequent repetition. You are like a good watch, which needs constant winding. Resume the books which moved you; they will do so again, and with greater profit than the first time. Bear with yourself, avoiding both self-deception and discouragement. This is a medium rarely attained; people either look complacently on themselves and their good intentions, or they despair utterly. Expect nothing of yourself, but all things of God. Knowledge of our own hopeless, incorrigible weakness, with unreserved confidence in God's Power, are the true foundations of all spiritual life. If you have not much time at your own disposal, do not fail to make good use of every moment you have. It does not need long hours to love God, to renew the consciousness of His Presence, to lift up the heart to Him or worship Him, to offer Him all we do or bear. This is the true Kingdom of God within us, which nothing can disturb.

XXII.

SUPPORT UNDER DIFFICULTY.

Nov. 4, 1692.

You need not doubt, Madame, as to what is your support under your difficulties. God is using them to detach you from yourself, and from the easy-going side of life. Recollection and fervour would do less to lower your pride and crucify your over-indulged senses. Endeavour voluntarily to make time for reading, prayer, solitude, and silence. Be firm! Deny yourself especially at night, so as to enable yourself to get more time in the morning; but when the order of Providence brings you unavoidable hindrances, do not be disturbed. Wheresoever God may lead you, there you will find Himself, as much in the most harassing business as in the calmest meditation.

And together with interior nourishment you will find self-mortification. . . . I pray God with all my heart that He may be your Light in the difficulties now surrounding you. Indeed, Madame, I often think of you, and the grace you stand in need of—often when, perhaps, you do not suppose I am heeding you. Nothing can exceed the earnest desire I have for your welfare.

XXIII.

PATIENCE UNDER GOD'S HAND.

Nov. 12, 1692.

I AM delighted to hear your good news of the Comte de Gramont, and wish him a long and happy life more than ever, since he seriously seeks to use it well. If I thought it would not disturb him to see me, I would try to steal away between our morning and evening lessons, and congratulate him on his good intentions. . . .

As to you, Madame, you can only bear your cross patiently. The trying things which you fancy come between God and you will prove means of union with Him if you bear them humbly. Those things which overwhelm us and upset our pride do more good than all which excites and inspirits us. You, more than most people, need to be overthrown like S. Paul at Damascus; you need to realise that you have no resource in yourself. The deeper the wound, so much the larger and more painful must the probing be. All that you are suffering comes of God's Hand healing you of a wound you recked not of, but which is a thousandfold worse than those natural sores which trouble you. Pride is fouler than this bodily abscess, though you are not so horrified at it. Do not be discouraged; give yourself up to God's Hand, Who is dealing with you in mercy—without by perplexity, and within by sickness. He loves you, and would have you love Him like our Lord upon His Cross. If you put no limit to what you expect of Him, it will be to you according to your faith.

XXIV.

ON THE COMTE DE GRAMONT'S RECOVERY.

VERSAILLES, Jan. 25, 1693.

I WAS very sorry, Madame, not to see you when you were last here. I hope the Comte de Gramont's good health will allow you to return soon for a longer time. I hear that his health is excellent; it is God's gift, and it would be unfair to use it against Him. The Comte must deal honourably and definitely with God, as he has ever dealt with those he encountered in the world; God loves a noble heart, and real nobility implies fidelity, firmness, and constancy. Could one so grateful to the King, whose gifts are perishable, be ungrateful and faithless to God, Who gives all things? I do not believe it, and will not suppose it possible. I think I know how good a heart the Comte has, and I reckon upon his courage in despising false shame and contemptible ridicule. . . . You, better than any one, Madame, can help him to guard against bad habits and the insidious entanglements of society. He should reflect seriously that his recovery, while deferring death, does but defer it, and that the longest life can be but short. But I do not mean to preach; I would rather rejoice with you over this welcome recovery. I long to see you both here in perfect health, and with the same earnest mind. I am, etc.

XXV.

GOD'S CROSSES SAFER THAN SELF-CHOSEN CROSSES.

Issy, May 25.

THE crosses which we make for ourselves by over-anxiety as to the future are not Heaven-sent crosses. We tempt God by our false wisdom, seeking to forestall His arrangements, and struggling to supplement His Providence by our own provisions. The fruit of our wisdom is always bitter. God suffers it to be so that we may be discomfited when we forsake His Fatherly guidance. The future is not ours: we may never have a future; or, if it comes, it may be wholly different to all we foresaw. Let us shut our eyes to that which God hides from us in the hidden depths of His Wisdom. Let us worship without seeing; let us be silent and lie still.

The crosses actually laid upon us always bring their own special grace and consequent comfort with them; we see the Hand of God when It is laid upon us. But the crosses wrought by anxious foreboding are altogether beyond God's dispensations; we meet them without the special grace adapted to the need—nay, rather in a faithless spirit, which precludes grace. And so everything seems hard and unendurable; all seems dark, helpless, and the soul which indulged in inquisitively tasting forbidden fruit finds nought save hopeless rebellion and death within. All this comes of not trusting to God, and prying into His hidden ways. "Sufficient unto the day is the evil thereof," our Lord has said, and the evil of each day becomes good if we leave it to God. What are we that we should ask Him, Why doest Thou thus? It is the Lord, and that is enough; it is the Lord, let Him do as seemeth Him good. Let Him lift up or cast down, let Him wound or heal, let Him smite or soothe, let Him give life or death, He is always Lord; we are but His work, a very toy in His Hand. What matter, so long as He is glorified, and His Will be fulfilled in us? Let us throw self aside, and then God's Will, unfolding hour by hour, will content us as to all He does in or around us. The contradictions of men, their inconstancy, their very injustice, will be seen to be the results of God's Wisdom, Justice, and unfailing Goodness; we shall see nought save that Infinitely Good God hidden behind the weakness of blind, sinful men.

Thus the deceitful course of this world, which flits before us like a stage scene, will become a very real thing, worthy of eternal praise. The greatest of men are nothing of themselves, but God is great in them. He uses their caprices, their pride, their dissimulation, vanity, and other wild passions, to set forward His everlasting purposes for His elect. He turns all within and without, the sins of others, our own failings, to our sanctification; all in Heaven and earth is designed to purify and make us worthy of Him. So let us be glad when our Heavenly Father tries us with sundry inward or outward temptations; when He surrounds us with external contrarieties and internal sorrow, let us rejoice, for thus our faith is tried as gold in the fire. Let us rejoice to learn the hollowness and unreality of all that is not God; it is this crucial experience which snatches us from self and the world. Let us rejoice, for by such travail the new man is born in us.

What! shall we be disheartened while God's Hand is hastening His work? We are perpetually calling on Him to do it, and so soon as He begins we are troubled, our cowardice and impatience hinder Him. I said that in the trials of life we learn the hollowness and falseness of all that is not God—hollowness, because there is nothing real where the One Sole Good is not; and falseness, because the world promises, kindles hopes, but gives nought save vanity and sorrow of heart—above all, in high places. Unreality must be unreal everywhere, but in high places it is all the worse because it is more decorated; it excites desire, kindles hope, and can never fill the heart. That which is itself empty cannot fill another. The weak, wretched idols of earth cannot impart a strength or happiness which they do not possess themselves. Do men seek to draw water from a dry well? Surely not. Then why should they look for peace and joy from great people who are ever complaining, who themselves cannot find amusement, and who are consumed with *ennui* amid all their outward display? "They that make them are like unto them," as the Prophet says of idolaters.[1] Let us fix our hopes higher, further from the casualties of this life.

Further, I said that all that is not God will be found to be vanity and falsehood, and consequently we find them in ourselves. What is so vain as our own heart? With what delusions do we not deceive ourselves? Happy he who is thoroughly undeceived, but our heart is as vain and false as the outer world; we must not despise that without despising ourselves. We are even worse than the world, because we have received greater things from God. Let us bear patiently if the world, with a hidden retribution, fails or misuses us, as we have so often failed or mistreated God, doing despite to His Spirit of Grace. The more the world disgusts us, the more it is furthering God's work, and while seeking to harm us it will help us.

I pray that you may daily grow in these truths, that they may take deep root in your heart, and specially help

[1] Ps. cxv. 8.

you to be renewed in the Spirit of Jesus Christ during your retreat. "May the Peace of God, which passeth all understanding, keep your heart and mind in Christ Jesus." Cut away every root of bitterness, and cast aside whatever disturbs the simple peace and trust of a child of God. Turn to your Father in every care; bury yourself in that tender Bosom, where nothing can fail you; rejoice in hope, and, casting aside the world and the flesh, taste the pure joys of the Holy Spirit. May your faith be unmoved amid every storm, and may you ever remember the words of the great Apostle, "All things work together for good to them that love God, to them who are called according to His purpose."[1]

XXVI.

PRACTICE OF RECOLLECTION AT BY-TIMES.

Nov. 17, 1694.

I THINK you should try, without any painful effort, to dwell upon God as often as a longing for recollection, and regret that you cannot cultivate it more, comes over you. It will not do to wait for disengaged seasons, when you can close your door and be alone. The moment in which we crave after recollection is that in which to practise it; turn your heart then and there to God,

[1] Rom. viii. 28.

simply, familiarly, and trustfully. The most interrupted seasons may be used thus; not merely when you are out driving, but when you are dressing, having your hair arranged—even when you are eating, and when others are talking. Useless and tiresome details in conversation will afford you similar opportunities: instead of wearying you, or exciting your ridicule, they will give you time for recollection; and thus all things turn to good for those who love God.

Another very important rule is to abstain from any fault whenever you perceive that you are about to commit it, and to bear the humiliation involved if you only discover it when committed. If you perceive the danger before committing it, beware of resisting God's Holy Spirit, Who is warning you, lest you extinguish Him within you. He is sensitively jealous; He must be hearkened to and followed. If He be grieved, He will withdraw; the least resistance wounds Him. Let everything in you yield to Him the moment He makes Himself felt. Faults committed through frailty or haste are nothing in comparison with those which close the ear to the Secret Voice of the Holy Spirit when it whispers within the soul.

As to faults which are not perceived till after they are committed, excitement and the vexation of wounded self-love will never make amends; on the contrary, such vexation is merely the impatience of pride at what is upsetting to it. So the only way to deal with such faults is to humble yourself quietly. I say quietly, because there can be no humility where there is irritation and vexation. You ought to condemn your fault, and accept your humiliation in God's Sight, without being irritated at yourself or disheartened, quietly making use of that humiliation. This is the way to win the antidote to the serpent's bite from itself. The shame of sin, borne without impatience, is the antidote of sin; but there is no humility in resisting the humiliation.

A passing thought of God during meal-times (especially when they are long, and with considerable intervals) will be very profitable in helping you to resist self-indulgence, and your exceeding fastidiousness. Besides, in the first hungry beginning of a meal there is often not much conversation, and then you can turn your thoughts to God. But all this should be done naturally as the inclination arises, and not constrainedly.... We often do not give God that which He asks of us; it is precisely what we are least willing to give, and we dread His asking it. He sternly requires Isaac, the only, the beloved son; all the rest is nothing in His Eyes, and He lets it be at once hard and profitless, because His Blessing is not upon a half-hearted offering. He wills to have all, and without all there is no rest to be found. "Who hath hardened himself against Him, and hath prospered?" we read in Holy Scripture.[1] If you would prosper, and have God's Blessing on your work, withhold nothing, cut to the quick, burn, spare not, and the God of Peace will be with you. Who can tell the comfort, the freedom, the strength, the influx of grace, when there is nothing left between God and the soul, and everything has been offered to Him, to the uttermost. I pray daily that God may give you strength to do this.

XXVII.

FAULTS TO BE MET WITH A VIGOROUS SPIRIT.

I DO not fully remember what I said that you wished to have in writing, but I think we were talking of an exceeding sensitiveness which cannot be controlled. Many people worry and torment themselves uselessly about this.

Such sensitiveness does not depend upon ourselves; God has given it as part of our disposition, as a trial, and He does not will to set us free, but rather to use it as a discipline. Be it ours to enter into His design. Temptations are necessary; our business is not to give way under them. Internal and external temptations alike all tend to strengthen us for victory. Interior temptations are the most profitable, because they humble

[1] Job ix. 4.

us more directly by showing us our inward corruption, while external temptations tend rather to show the wickedness of the world around us. But our inward temptations make us feel that our own natural inclinations are as bad as those of the world itself. All alike come from God's Hand, Who can use both ourselves and others to teach us self-mortification.

Not unfrequently it is the revolt of pride, which is disturbed and disheartened at seeing such internal rebellion just when it would fain find submission, and be able to indulge self-complacency. We must strive to be faithful in will, notwithstanding our natural repugnances and opposition; we must not resist God when He pleases to show us by these tempests to what shipwreck we are exposed did not His Hand save us. Even if we should fall deliberately through weakness, we must humble and correct ourselves without giving way to self-pity. We must not lose a moment in returning to God; only we must do so naturally and without excitement, rising up and resuming our course vigorously, without being mortified and disappointed at our fall.

XXVIII.

FREEDOM FROM SELF.

So long as we are centred in self, we shall be a prey to the contradiction, the wickedness, and injustice of men.

Our temper brings us into collision with other tempers; our passions clash with those of our neighbours; our wishes are so many tender places open to the shafts of those around; our pride, which is incompatible with our neighbours', rises like the waves of a stormy sea;—everything rouses, attacks, rebuffs us. We are exposed on all sides by reason of the sensitiveness of passion and the jealousy of pride. No peace is to be looked for within when we are at the mercy of a mass of greedy, insatiable longings, and when we can never satisfy that "me" which is so keen and so touchy as to whatever concerns it. Hence in our dealings with others we are like a bed-ridden invalid, who cannot be touched anywhere without pain. A sickly self-love cannot be touched without screaming; the mere tip of a finger seems to scarify it. Then add to this the roughness of neighbours in their ignorance of self, their disgust at our infirmities (at the least as great as ours towards theirs), and you soon find all the children of Adam tormenting one another, each embittering the other's life. And this martyrdom of self-love you will find in every nation, every town, every community, every family, often between friends.

The only remedy is to renounce self. If we set aside—lose sight of—self, we shall have nothing to lose, to fear, or to consider; and then we shall find that true peace which is given to "men of good-will," *i.e.* those who have no will save God's, which has become theirs. Then men will not be able to harm us; they can no longer attack us through hopes or fears, for we shall be ready for everything, and refuse nothing. And this is to be inaccessible, invulnerable to the enemy. Man can only do what God permits, and whatever God permits him to do against us becomes our will, because it is God's. So doing, we shall store our treasure so high that no human hand can reach to assail it. Our good name may be tarnished, but we consent, knowing that if God humbles us, it is good to be humbled. Friendship fails us : well! it is because the One True Friend is jealous of all others, and sees fit to loosen our ties. We may be worried, inconvenienced, distressed; but it is God, and that is enough. We love the Hand which smites; there is peace beneath all our woes, a blessed peace. We will that which is, we desire nothing which is denied us; and the more absolute this self-renunciation, the deeper our peace. Any lingering wishes and clingings disturb it; if every bond were broken, our freedom would be boundless. Let contempt, pain, death, overwhelm me, still I hear Jesus Christ saying, "Fear not them which kill the body, but are not able to kill the soul."[1] Powerless indeed are they; even though they can destroy life, their day is soon over! They can but break the earthen vessel, kill that which voluntarily dies daily. Anticipate somewhat the welcome deliverance, and then the soul

[1] Matt. x. 28.

will escape from their hands into the Bosom of God, where all is unchanging peace and rest.

XXIX.

TO THE COMTESSE DE MONTBERON.[1]
ON A SIMPLE MIND.

YOUR religion is somewhat too restless and active. Do not distrust God; so long as you do not fail Him He will not fail you, but will give you such help as you need to serve Him. Either His Providence will supply you with external guidance, or His Holy Spirit will make up within for that which is outwardly lacking. Believe that God is faithful to His promises, and He will give you according to the measure of your faith. If you were forsaken in a desert wilderness, manna would fall from Heaven for you alone, and waters would gush forth from the rocks. So fear nothing save mistrust of God, and do not be over-anxious even on that score. Bear with yourself as you would bear with others, without self-deception. Put aside all your mental and spiritual fastidiousness, which you are disposed to display towards God as well as to men. There is a great deal of refined selfishness and complacency in all that. Be natural with Him Who delights to reveal Himself to the simple heart. Become

[1] The following letters, to No. LXV., are all addressed to this lady.

common; not by vulgarity, but by renouncing all fastidiousness of intellect. "Blessed are the poor in spirit;"— who have taken the vow of spiritual poverty, who live from day to day by continual alms, and by absolute self-surrender to Providence! How glad I should be to see you as indifferent about intellectual things as a penitent is about dress and ornaments!

XXX.

SOME RULES AS TO DRESS.

You are not mistaken, Madame, in believing that it is not enough merely to change the object of eagerness, and that there is a restless eagerness which needs checking, even in God's service, and the correction of our own faults. This thought may be of great use in calming without relaxing your energy. The eagerness with which you set about the best things mars them, and throws you into an excitement which is all the more opposed to the peacefulness of God's Holy Spirit because you strive to control it, and hide it within you out of mere worldly courtesy. A little simplicity would enable you to exercise the same virtue with less effort.

I highly approve of your communicating once a fortnight. It is not too often for one leading a retired life, trying to give herself to her duties, to reading and prayer.

You need to seek food, comfort, and strength to bear your crosses, and overcome your failings in the Sacrament of love and life. Do not try to judge yourself, or give way to any scruples as to your communion.

As to confession, I can say nothing, only your Confessor can speak positively as to that. God will not suffer him to fail you if you strive simply to do that which His Grace requires of you. Go on in full, hearty faith, and try to do as your Confessor bids you.

Neither can I say anything very definite as to your reading and prayer. I do not know enough of your tastes, leadings, or needs. . . .

As to dress, it seems to me you ought to consider M. de Montberon's tastes and wishes. If he thinks economy necessary, you should retrench as much as possible; if he wishes you to keep up a certain external style, do whatever he seems to desire, simply to please him, not to indulge your own tastes. If he leaves you to your own judgment in this matter, I should say that a medium was the best self-denial for you. You are inclined to extremes; your pride and fastidiousness would stop short in nothing but perfect magnificence;—and severe simplicity is but another refinement of self-will; it is a splendid renunciation of splendour. But the mid-course is trying to pride. It makes you seem wanting in taste, and feel commonplace. I have heard of you formerly dressing like the Sisters of a Community; this is too much outwardly, and too little in reality. Moderation in dress will be a much greater trial to you in the bottom of your heart; but your unfailing rule should be perfect openness with M. de Montberon, and unhesitating compliance with whatever you see pleases him best.

XXXI.

ON MEDITATION.

April 15, 1700.

As to meditation, use it not merely at appointed times, but further, in the intervals between other occupations as much as you find yourself able; but be careful to husband your strength, bodily and mental, and stop whenever you feel weary. Always begin with the most weighty points which have struck you when reading. Follow the leadings of your heart, so as to sustain yourself with a loving realisation of God's Presence, of the Holy Trinity, and of the Incarnation of Jesus Christ. Cling closely to this holy companionship, give yourself up to it with boundless confidence, and hold such converse with it as a single-hearted love inspires. When you have spoken out of the abundance of your heart to those Blessed Ones, hearken with your mental ear, silencing your restless, eager spirit. As to distractions, they will die away of themselves if you never encourage them voluntarily, if you choose the path of love, if you are not distracted by the fear of distractions, and if, when you find your imagination wandering, you recall it quietly and without vexation to your devotions. Your facility in meditation is a token of God's Love; for, were it otherwise, your scrupulous temperament would disturb you greatly when you want to think upon God.

As to reading, I am not afraid of your studying most parts of Holy Scripture. . . . I specially advise you to read the New Testament, but do not dwell upon the difficult passages of the Epistle to the Romans; also the historical books of the Old Testament, the Psalms, Proverbs, Wisdom, and Ecclesiasticus, and parts of the Prophecies. Do not forget the *Imitation of Christ*, or S. Francis de Sales' Works. His *Letters* and his *Entretiens* are full of teaching and experience. When what you read induces meditation, put down the book, and resume it afterwards. Read but little at once; read slowly and quietly; read lovingly.

Do not dwell any more on your general confessions; it is a danger to the peace which God would give you, and might rekindle your scruples. Whatever excites your sensitive, eager thoughts is a peril and a snare to you. Follow trustfully the attraction God gives you towards His Infinite Perfection. Love Him as you wish to be loved; it is none too much. Love Him according to the notions He has given you of exceeding love. Do not make yourself a martyr to *les bienséances*, and to perfect courtesy. Such sensitiveness consumes the mind, and involves too much self-concentration. Speak and act without so much circumspection. If you are absorbed in God, you will be less eager to please men, and will really please them more.

XXXII.

ON THE SICKNESS OF A FRIEND.

June 13, 1700.

I SYMPATHISE sincerely in the grief which the dangerous illness of Mdlle. . . . causes you, and your suspense is a still further trial. Nothing is so trying to nature as suspense between a faint hope and a mighty fear; but we must have faith as to the extent of our trials, as in all else. Our sensitiveness makes us often disposed to fancy that we are tried beyond our strength, but we really know neither our strength to endure nor the nature of God's trials. Only He Who knows both these, and every turn of the hearts which He has made, knows how to deal out a due proportion. Let us leave it all to Him, and be content to bear in silence. What we call impossible is only such to our softness and cowardice; what we fancy overwhelming is only so to pride and self-will, which cannot be too much crushed. But the new Adam finds fresh strength and heavenly consolation in this crushing of the old Adam.

Offer up your friend to God; would you withhold her from Him? Would you put her between Him and you, as a wall of separation? What do you sacrifice but the short, wretched life of a person who could only suffer and, perhaps, risk her salvation here? You will soon see her again, not in this world's sunshine, which lights up nought save vanity and sorrow, but in the pure light of eternal truth, which blesses all those who behold it. The more upright and excellent your friend, the fitter she is not to tarry in this evil world. It is true that there are but few real friends, and it is hard to lose them; but we do not lose them—we rather are in danger of losing ourselves while waiting to follow those we mourn.

As to prayer, Madame, do not fear. There is no illusion in following God's leading, and abiding in His Presence engrossed in love and admiration, provided such engrossment never gives us a foolish idea that we are very advanced; provided it does not prevent our being conscious of frailty, imperfection, and the need of amendment; provided it never leads us to neglect any duty, external or internal; provided we are sincere, humble, simple, and docile to those set over us. Do not hesitate; accept God's gifts. Open your heart to Him, feed upon Him. Hesitation would constrain you, interfere with the workings of grace, and plunge you into a sea of perplexities, in which you would always be undoing with one hand what the other does. So long as you think of God, love Him, abide in His Presence, and cleave to His Will without presumption, without neglecting any duty or relaxing in precept or counsel, without wandering from obedience and the ordinary path, you will be in no danger of delusion. Follow God's leadings. Say to the Bridegroom, "Draw me, and I will run after Thee."[1] Put no limit to your recollection, save what is requisite to preserve health, and to fulfil the duties of your position in life. Only, take care that your body does not suffer from your mind's activity. . . . I should fear this more than illusion in a life so upright and regular as yours.

XXXIII.

ON THE DEATH OF THE SAME.

June 23, 1790.

I WAITED for you to hear from others of your friend's death. God has taken her from this world's perils, after preparing her by long sickness, and He has deprived you of

[1] Cant. i. 4.

a very excellent friend who satisfied your fastidious taste. All that He does seems hard, but it is in mercy. Soon all this will be over, and we shall see in the light of truth how well God loves us when He lays the cross upon us.

XXXIV.

THE BEGINNINGS OF DIVINE LOVE.

July 26, 1700.

I AM very irregular, but you require my irregularities and my dryness. Until our friends become perfect we must turn their imperfections to good account; they will be more profitable than even perfections if they mortify and detach us. So forgive me all my faults, and believe me when I say with all Christian sincerity that no one can care for you more heartily and stedfastly than I do.

You are still in swaddling-clothes; but as children grow these are loosened. There is one kind of growth, however, which I do not covet for you. God forbid that you should grow after the world's fashion. Jesus Christ would not allow His full-grown Apostles to keep little children from coming to Him; the Kingdom of Heaven is theirs, He said, and woe to the great who do not become small like them. I infinitely prefer your swaddling-clothes and your childlike timidity to the stiff, proud dignity of strict Pharisees.

When God moulds a soul to Himself, it readily dispenses with whatever externals He takes away. Love is a great casuist in all doubtful matters; it possesses a delicacy and jealous perception which exceeds all human reasoning. We ought to be subject to external order, and submit to those set over us; but when externals are lacking, we must sit loose to them, live by faith, and be led by love. . . . What you experience is a great novelty for you; it is an altogether unknown life to you. One does not know one's self; one seems to be dreaming with one's eyes open. Receive all, but set your heart on nothing; love, bear, and still love on. Dwell little on your gifts, save to thank the Bridegroom Who gives them; be very simple, docile, faithful to duty in every detail. Love imparts great freedom; it makes everything simple without despising rule.

Take as much sleep as you can, your body needs it; and you must not neglect that, even out of eagerness for prayer. The spirit of prayer knows how even to leave off praying when it is in conformity to God's requirements. While you sleep your heart will watch. When sleepless, do not fail to recall God's Presence, but you must not sacrifice needful sleep. What you are now feeling is but the beginning. The most vivid and excited feelings are not the purest or deepest; but the keenness of newborn love sows the first seeds within the heart.

Be it yours now to draw the sweet milk of love from the fount of Divine Compassion; love even as God prompts you at the present moment. By and by, if He imposes privation on you, your love will change its character, and you will experience another kind of novelty.

XXXV.

SCRUPLES.

Sept. 2, 1700.

. . . I WISH you were as simple in your confessions as in meditation. But God works gradually, and the slowness with which He works tends to humble us, to exercise our patience as regards ourselves, and to make us more dependent on Him. So we must wait patiently for your simplicity to grow and spread over your confessions, in which I can see that you indulge too much scruple. There is no objection to your communicating on the appointed days without going to confession, when you have no definite fault of which to accuse yourself since your last confession. This may easily occur in the short interval between your confessions. God would have us enjoy liberty when we seek Him only. Love is familiar; it has no reservations, no contrivances; it lies on the surface of all intercourse with the Beloved. Where we find scrupulous consideration about

Him, we must suspect that some other love divides the heart, restraining it, and causing it to hesitate. We do not dwell so much and so anxiously on our own state save because we are clinging to some other affection, and so put a limit on union with the Beloved. You who are so keenly alive to friendship, would you not feel the reserve of a friend towards whom you had none, especially if he were always doling out his confidence as though afraid of letting it exceed a certain limit? You would assuredly say, "I do not treat you as you treat me; I weigh nothing, and you weigh everything; you do not love me as I love you, or as you ought to love." And if you, all unworthy as you are, demand so single and unreserved a love, how much more right has the Heavenly Bridegroom to be jealous? Strive, then, to attain greater singleness of heart. I do not want anything which perplexes or constrains you; enough if you do not resist the leadings of simplicity, and if you throw aside all anxious retrospection when you discover it.

Follow the bent of your heart as to reading, and as to meditation do not waken the Bride until she awakes spontaneously. Take care of your health; let your imagination and senses have some diversion when you feel that they need external relief. Such innocent recreation will in nowise interfere with the loving Presence of God. . . . I will never fail you, please God.

I am dry and hard, but God lets His Own Goodness tell in those whom He uses to do His work, and who require tenderness to promote it. Trust yourself to God, and look to Him only. He is the real Friend, Whose Heart will always be infinitely tenderer than yours. Mistrust yourself, not Him. He is jealous, but it is the jealousy of exceeding Love, and we ought to be jealous over ourselves on His behalf, even as He is. Trust to love; it takes all, but it gives all. It leaves nothing in the heart save itself. It can tolerate nothing else; but then it can satiate every longing, for it comprises everything. Those who taste it are inebriate with a sweetness which yet is but a foretaste of heavenly joy. Conscious love ravishes, transports, absorbs, makes the soul indifferent to the loss of all else; but hidden love, which conceals itself to teach the soul detachment, is a sorer martyrdom than anything conceivable which is merely exterior.

XXXVI.

THE SOURCE OF SCRUPLES.

Nov. 7, 1700.

... I THOUGHT in our last conversation that your scruples had somewhat hindered and withered you. They would damage you irreparably if you listen to them; it would be real faithlessness. You are enlightened enough to let them go; and if you fail to do so, you will grieve the Holy Spirit of God. "Where the Spirit of the Lord is, there is liberty;"[1] but where constraint, anxiety, and a slavish fear are, there is self-will and overweening care for self. How far from all these disturbances true Love is. They who are so absorbed in their own fancies care but little for the Beloved. All your troubles come from want of faith. If you had not resisted God to follow your own devices, you would not have suffered thus; there is no greater evil than these efforts to attain a visionary relief. A dropsical patient only increases his thirst by drinking, and so the victim of scruples only increases his trouble by heeding them; and indeed he deserves it. The only cure is to silence them and turn at once to God; and at such times it is prayer and not confession that will heal the heart. Try, then, to make up for lost time; for, honestly, I think you are rather upset and enfeebled. But this evil may be turned to good; for such experience of privation, of trial, and of your own weakness, will carry light with it, and teach you not to think too much of the pleasant side of your more peaceful and abounding phases. Take heart, and be very straightforward; you are not enough so, and that often makes you argue, and prevents your speaking out fully.

[1] 2 Cor. iii. 17.

XXXVII.

DANGER OF SCRUPLES.

Dec. 12, 1700.

I OFTEN apply the words to you, "As water puts out fire, so scruples put out the spirit of prayer." Do not indulge your scruples so much, and you will be at rest. There are two things which ought to clear away all your fears. One is the consciousness of your excitability, and your skilfulness in tormenting yourself about nothing. You have often perceived it; all your spiritual guides have convicted you of it. It was a recognised temptation before you began to practise meditation, and that cannot have increased it. To meditate profitably, you must cast aside your scruples as old temptations which you have been always told not to encourage. Meditation does not make that which was innocent bad or dangerous; it does not prove your former Directors wrong in what they all decided upon, independently of such matters.

The second thing which ought to satisfy you is the harm which these scruples do you. Every time that, contrary to your own good sense and to obedience, you begin again with those self-investigations so often forbidden you, you distract and perplex yourself; you get farther from the power of prayer, and so from God; you fall back into your natural difficulties; you rekindle your old troubles, your fastidiousness and other faults; you become almost entirely self-absorbed. Now, I ask you, is all this of God? is it by following the eadings of His Grace that you wander so far from Him? When I returned, I found you so depressed, so ready to break down altogether, that I hardly knew you. Is that God's doing? Do you trace His Hand in it? Does love make us leave off loving? Moreover, in the simple, regular life you have led since you began to meditate more, you can only recall trifling faults. Is it not wrong in God's Sight to forsake close communing with Him in prayer in order to indulge an anxious search after all these trifles, which you magnify in your imagination? Let us take them at their worst, and grant them to be real sins; at any rate they can only be venial sins, for which you should humble yourself, and strive diligently to correct them, but which a loving prayer will readily blot out. What you need is to turn your scrupulous sensitiveness chiefly against your very scruples. Can it be right, under pretext of hunting out the smallest faults, to dry up the sources of prayer, and to do one's self so much harm in order to remedy so little? I am not referring to the present moment; just now you do not need such exhortations, but the need may recur at any time. Scruples are an illusion as to evil just as much as unreal prayer is an illusion concerning what is good. All such prayer as calms and sustains the soul, which humbles and detaches it, which only flags when scruples intervene, and which is only lost by losing love, can but be good. There can be no illusion in believing without seeing, in loving without selfishness, in receiving without stopping short in what is given, in renouncing all that is of self, in act or will.

XXXVIII.

LOVE OF GOD THE ANTIDOTE TO SCRUPLES.

Dec. 26, 1700.

You are not mistaken in thinking that the exaltation which comes of love does not puff up. It is a token which may reassure one as to any danger of illusion. Our inmost experience teaches us that love comes infinitely more from God than from ourselves; the love that fills our hearts is God's own creation. It is a somewhat which is our very life, and which yet is altogether superior to us; we can take no credit to ourselves from it. The more we love God, the more we feel that He is at once the Lover and the Beloved. Verily, those who love truly are little disposed to any self-complacency because of it! Love is but a borrowed treasure; we feel that it does all, and that were it not given us we could do nothing. If I strove to love in my own strength, what should I love but myself? God, in His All-wise adaptation, never gives the highest love without its makeweight. We feel two altogether opposite elements within us—an overwhelming weakness and imperfection in all that is of us, and a borrowed transport of love so out of proportion to all the rest, that we cannot take credit to ourselves for it. If you lift a child up on high, so far from imagining itself to have attained a great height, it is terrified lest it fall, unless you hold it tight in its exalted position. Love is the real source of humility, for it abases all save the Beloved; it so engrosses us with Him, that we altogether forget self; it sets something so far beyond our nature before us, that we learn to appreciate our own worthlessness and want of strength.

Persevere with your communions. Scrupulous consciences need to be urged onwards, like restive, shying horses. The more you yield to your scruples, the more you develop them. You can only cure them by repression; and as you conquer them you will gain peace and rest. Moreover, this will not be mere peace, but an enlightened state, which will enable you clearly to perceive where the snare of your scruple lies, and which will bring forth good fruit. This will be a token that God is leading you. Nothing is so hurtful to simplicity as a scrupulous mind; it is a cloak for all manner of falseness and duplicity. We fancy that all our anxiety arises from our sensitive love of God, but really there is a great deal of self-seeking in it, of jealous study of our own perfection, of natural self-interest. We deceive ourselves to our own discomfort, and turn aside from God under pretext of caution.

XXXIX.

HOW THE LOVE OF GOD LIGHTENS SUFFERING.

Jan. 5, 1701.

I SYMPATHISE, Madame, with your invaild's sufferings, but I rejoice that she bears them so well. Do you remember a passage in *Le Chrétien Intérieur:*[1] "They who reject suffering do not love, for love is ever ready to suffer for the Beloved One"? You are not wrong in distinguishing between willingness and courage. Courage is a sort of strength and vigour of mind by which we overcome everything; but souls which God intends to keep lowly, and conscious of their own weakness, do all that is allotted them without any sense of their own capability to do it. They feel as if everything were too much for them, yet they triumph over all difficulties by a *je ne sais*

---

[1] A book written somewhere between 1640-50 by M. de Bernières Louvigny.

quoi, which springs up altogether independently of themselves when needed, and for which they never dream of taking credit to themselves. They do not lay themselves out to suffer well, but somehow we find that each cross as it comes has been bravely borne, because they have had no will save God's. There is nothing striking, nothing powerful, nothing very obvious even to others, still less to themselves. If you say to such a person that he has endured bravely, he would not understand you. He does not know how it has all been; he does not dissect his feelings. If he did, there would be no more simplicity. This is what you mean by *willingness*, which makes less show, but is really much more solid than what is generally called courage. Good water has no smell; the purer it is the less it tastes. It is colourless; its purity makes it transparent, and consequently you see the colour of all extraneous matter thrown into it. So willingness, which is really love of God, has no colour of its own, only at every call it is ready to will whatever God wills. Happy they who have ever so small a seed of so great a blessing!

It is your task to foster and mould gradually this new life in one so dear to you. Do not hurry or forestall anything, but go on step by step as God leads; He will give the signals, be it yours to watch heedfully, and to shun alike negligence or politic reserve and eager haste.

XL.

CARE OF HEALTH AND DUTY.

Jan. 28, 1701.[1]

IF you are poorly, Madame, rest yourself, and do not go out. The good Saint we love so well will be with you by your own fireside. You know how he adapted himself to every weakness of mind or body. Love is love everywhere, and bodily weakness does not lessen the heart's warmth. Love is never so powerful as when resting on the Bosom of the Beloved. It seems that you have done too much on your journey; natural energy and eagerness have led you to overstep your physical power. Man may praise you for it, but God likes simpler, less ambitious proceedings. If you feel unequal to going to Mass to-morrow, give it up cheerfully, and be sure that if S. Francis de Sales were still among us, and your Director, he would certainly forbid you to go. He forbids you yet where he is. You will obey his mind in abstaining from the celebration of his fête-day. If you feel really fit to go to church, only remain during one Mass; but mistrust yourself, and condemn yourself not to go if there is any doubt in the matter.

[1] S. Francis de Sales' festival-day.

XLI.

PATIENCE WITH SELF.

Feb. 19, 1701.

PEOPLE who love themselves aright, even as they ought to love their neighbour, bear charitably, though without flattery, with self as with another. They know what needs correction at home as well as elsewhere; they strive heartily and vigorously to correct it, but they deal with self as they would deal with some one else they wished to bring to God. They set to work patiently, not exacting more than is practicable under present circumstances from themselves any more than from others, and not being disheartened because perfection is not attainable in a day. Such people judge their most trivial failings unsparingly, and are not blind to their own deformity, but endure all the mortification and humiliation involved. They neglect no means of amendment, but they are not fretful while so doing. They do not heed the pettishness of pride and self-esteem, which so often mingles with that quiet resolution wherewith grace inspires us for the correction of our faults. That sort of irritable pettishness only discourages a man, makes him self-absorbed, repels him from God's service, wearies him in his way, makes him seek unworthy consolations, dries him up, distracts, exhausts him, fills him with disgust and despair of ever reaching his end. Nothing so hinders souls as this inward peevishness when it is encouraged; but if endured without consenting to it, it may be turned to good, like all other trials by which God purifies and perfects us. The only thing to be done is to let such troubles pass away, like a headache or a feverish attack, without doing anything to promote or prolong them.

Meanwhile, it is well to go on with your interior practices and your exterior duties as far as possible. Prayer may be less easy, the Presence of God less evident and less comforting, outward duties may be harder and less acceptable, but the faithfulness which accomplishes them is greater, and that is enough for God. A boat which makes a quarter of a mile against wind and tide requires greater power on the part of the rowers than when it makes a mile with both favourable. The vexations of self-esteem should be treated as some men treat their nervous fancies, taking no notice of them any more than if they did not exist.

XLII.

EVIL OF SCRUPLES.

March 3, 1701.

I AM sorry for you, and not at all inclined to scold you, but I wish you would correspond faithfully to what God appears to require of you. The matters with which you reproach yourself, and speak of with such horror, are mere trivialities of talk, devoid of all malice, and perfectly harmless to your neighbours. Surely there is nothing in these to trouble you so much? These trifles rouse your scruples; your restless scruples disturb your prayer, draw you away from God, wither and distract your soul, open the door to earthly inclinations, and waken temptations in spite of grace. See how much worse the remedy is than the disease; the disease is imaginary, but the remedy is a real evil.

I am not surprised that your too lively imagination, and the habit of giving way to wandering thoughts, which you have never checked sufficiently, should trouble you; but it is not too late to overcome these hindrances in your heavenward path. At all events, you ought to be on the guard against your imagination, realise the harm it does, acknowledge how it engrosses you with trifles, which hide more important things; and, above all, you ought to be docile, and persevere in following the advice given you. So far from giving you up, I intend to persecute you unremittingly. I am not going to be discouraged by all your scruples; do not you lose courage to fight them. I most earnestly wish you to communicate to-morrow without going to confession. You will be wanting in your duty to God if you do not do as I ask you in His Name, and for love of Him.

XLIII.

FOREBODINGS TO BE AVOIDED.

CAMBRAI, *June* 10, 1701.

I HAD hoped, Madame, to find you here, and was rejoicing in that hope, but God has sent you elsewhere. Well, the best place is wherever He sends one, and any other would be undesirable, all the more because it was our own choice. . . . I am glad that the spiritual guide you have found seems likely to help you. I like and esteem him much, and am certain he might often do you good; but I do not mean to give you up myself. We were brought together by God, and so our union must last. I see nothing likely to remove me from hence, and there is no foundation at all for what you heard. So do not dwell upon these unlikely events; such forebodings as to the future are not wholesome for you. When God sends you help, try to see Him only in it, and take such help from day to day, as the Israelites their manna, without anxious thought for the morrow's provision.

Two things are essential to the life of pure faith: first, it teaches you always to see God behind all the frail agents He uses; and next, it keeps the soul ever in a state of suspense. One is, so to say, always in mid-air, without being able to touch the ground; one can never calculate from moment to moment on the help that will be given. We must leave to God whatever depends upon Him, and only try to be faithful in whatever depends upon ourselves. This dependence from hour to hour, this shadow, this calm amid uncertainty, is a silent but real martyrdom—like that of a slow fire. It is so slow and interior, that it is almost as imperceptible, even to the soul which endures it, as to those without. When God takes away that which once He gave you, He knows very well how to replace it, either through other means or by Himself. He is able to raise up children to Abraham from the stones.[1] When S. Paul the Hermit was in a solitary desert, a raven brought him half a loaf daily. If the Saint had been mistrustful, and wanted to secure his next day's bread, perhaps the raven would not have returned. Do you eat your half loaf quietly as your raven brings it. "The morrow shall take thought for

[1] Luke iii. 8.

the things of itself. Sufficient unto the day is the evil thereof."[1] He Who feeds you to-day will feed you to-morrow; and manna will fall again, as in the desert, before God's children will be left hungry.

XLIV.

HOW TO ACCEPT ENCOURAGEMENT.

June 16, 1701.

I AM delighted to hear that you are tranquil and happy, but beware of saying in your inward prosperity, "I shall never be removed."[2] If we are proud of our borrowed treasures, the lender is wont to overthrow the ungrateful borrower. Profit by your prosperity without treating it as your own merit. . . . Do nothing which can injure your weak health. As to your fear of comfort, you carry it too far: accept simply whatever is sent you, certain that you will be corrected if you do not use it soberly. There is a sort of self-will and self-seeking in rejecting the consolations God gives you, because they may involve certain temptations. It is like choosing for one's self, and rejecting a duty because of its responsibilities.

[1] Matt. vi. 34.   [2] Ps. xxx. 6.

XLV.

DISCRETION IN PRACTICE.

July 11, 1701.

THE words, "he whom Thou lovest is sick," rise to my mind. You are indeed very dear to me, and I want to see you well. I am afraid that you have exhausted yourself for want of care; indeed I have heard of your practising certain austerities. If you have done so without advice it is self-will, and it is far more important to mortify your self-will than your already feeble body. I beg you to husband your strength. . . .

July 30.

I am very anxious about you. You are expending your strength in various ways, which are all unacceptable to God, inasmuch as they are acts of disobedience. You deprive yourself of consolation of which God would not deprive you; and it is as wrong to take away what He does not take away, as to appropriate what He denies. Moreover, you are eaten up with scruples, which leave you no peace or rest, no breathing time; and meanwhile they hamper you with a perpetual confession of trifles, enough to drive both yourself and your confessor wild. Only obedience can put an end to such a wrong state of things: this you will not practise, and I honestly tell you I am displeased with you. If you were more simple-hearted you would obey without arguing or self-pleasing. Childlike hearts hold their tongue, and do as they are bid; real love does not know what it is to falter in obedience. The same thing which undermines your health will sap your interior life and leave you a prey to fancies, unrestrained by docility; and I suffer from seeing you suffering thus in defiance of God's Will. I will have nothing to do with your spiritual guidance unless you promise—*1st*, To do whatever you are bid as to taking more sleep and nourishment; *2nd*, to follow P. R.'s rules as to your confession; and *3rd*, to make use of such comforts and alleviations as are suitable in a spirit of simplicity. I must have a speedy, frank, and decided answer. God knows how much you grieve me.

XLVI.

DANGERS OF A SELF-TORMENTING SPIRIT.

Aug. 1 *to* 25, 1701.

IF I speak harshly, you must remember what I have learnt by experience. Gentle words are not strong enough to repress your scruples, but you know that I am far from wishing to deal harshly with you. Am I to let you waste inwardly and outwardly through scruples? ...

Docility would be the remedy for all your ills, but self-will makes all remedies useless. You seem to have a bandage over your eyes, so that you do not see how scrupulous you ought to be as to these useless scruples, instead of blinding yourself to a disobedience which is altogether opposed to God's Mind.

. . . I must beg you to stay in bed as long as formerly, and to try to recover the power of sleep which you have lost. It will return if you are patient and quiet, but giving way to imagination you banish it more and more. I shall not be satisfied as to your inward state until you possess your soul in patience, and sleep quietly. I only want calmness and docility. You will say that a calm imagination does not depend upon ourselves. Pardon me, it does to a great degree. When we have set aside all voluntary disturbances, we go a long way to diminish those which are involuntary. A little stone dropped into the water disturbs it for long, and it is not easy to stop the commotion; but leave it alone, and gradually the commotion will cease of itself. God will watch over your imagination, if you do not keep up disturbance by your scrupulous reflections.

. . . I would fain only comfort you, but I must begin with scolding; you really need it. . . . If you go on following your own way, you will consume your heart and lose ground day by day; if you heed God's Voice speaking through those who are His representatives to you, peace will return. "Who hath hardened himself against God, and hath prospered?"[1] You chose to take what God refused, and presumptuously to refuse what He did not refuse, because it was necessary to you. You were like a baby who should refuse its milk, and cry for dry bread before it has teeth to bite. Return to the pure milk of Divine Consolation: "Taste and see how gracious the Lord is."

. . . You are wasting your strength, bodily and mental. It is merely your restlessness which hinders your peace and inward sweetness. How can you hear God's gentle Voice pleading with your soul when you are making so much noise with your wayward imagination? Hush that, and God will make Himself heard. . . . Your husband seems to think that reading S. Teresa had revived your scruples—you see what harm your restless activity may do. You ask for consolation; why, you are standing on the fountain's edge, though you will not stoop to drink! Peace and comfort will only be found in obedience. You will receive according to your faith,—much if you believe fervently, nothing if you go on heeding your foolish fancies, which will multiply indefinitely. . . . You do dishonour to real love, making it seem to be always engrossed with trifles, whereas it really goes straight to God

[1] Job ix. 4.

in the fullest simplicity. . . . I pray God to teach you the truth of David's words, " I will run the way of Thy commandments, when Thou hast set my heart at liberty."[1]

XLVII.

SELF-WILL IN RELIGIOUS EXERCISES.

Feb. 15, 1702.

I AM unwilling to agitate you in your present state, but I must put before you the fact that, as a matter of conscience, you ought to give up the comfort of going to church on week days. I hear that you go twice a day, and that at a time when M. Bourdon [the physician] does not hesitate to say that you are not fit to leave your room, or even your bed! I cannot doubt M. Bourdon's great skill, or his sincerely conscientious piety; he does not come to his conclusions from what you say, but from what he sees. . . . Even if he were mistaken you ought to abide by his decision. It is a matter which is not precept, and you would not be guilty even of the slightest venial sin in obeying him. . . . Even if you fancy you know best, you ought to mistrust yourself. Is it not better to obey your skilful doctor, your very pious husband, and your pastor, who knows you thoroughly? If you do not, you will be guilty of the greatest presumption, preferring

[1] Ps. cxix. 32.

your own opinion to God's providential ordering, and to the lawful authority of the superiors God has set over you. What can you answer if God were to say: "Your superiors decided, and you told them all your reasons; they weighed them, and thought them insufficient; but you persisted in disobedience, you preferred your scruples to obedience and submission; you have killed yourself by self-will?"

[The remainder of this letter is missing.]

XLVIII.

GOD'S GIFTS TO BE WELCOMED, FROM WHATEVER SOURCE.

March 18, 1702.

... You see what God requires of you: can you refuse? You see that your resistance is but a refinement of self-love: dare you oppose such refinements, such subtle self-seeking to His Mercy? You who indulge such scruples about some involuntary, and consequently innocent, thought,—you who constantly confess things which are no matter for confession,—can you entertain no scruple, see no need to confess a prolonged resistance to God's Holy Spirit through a mere fancy of self-will, which rejects God's Gifts, unless they happen to come through the channel which pleases you? What matter indeed if you received the gifts of grace as hungry beggars receive bread? Those gifts would but be purer and more precious. Your heart would be more worthy of God, if its humility and self-abnegation won the help God sends. Is this how you put aside self? how you accept God's dealings in simple faith? how you die to self and pride? What good do all your books about pure love, all your frequent meditations, do you? how can you read what condemns you so utterly? Not merely self-will, but a refined spirit of pride overpowers you, and makes you reject God's Gift, because it does not come in a fashion pleasing to your fastidiousness. How can you pray? What does God whisper in the loving silence of the soul? does He not ask death to self, and you seek to make it live? Can you say to Him, "I will have nothing of Thy Goodness unless Thou wilt give it through some one who altogether satisfies the foolish fancies of my heart?" Dare you say, "I am jealous?" Will He not answer, "I too am jealous, but jealousy beseems Me only, and thine must be swallowed up of Mine?"

O my God, recall this wandering soul; show her the horrible danger of her temptation. Teach her to be jealous for Thee, not for herself; strip her of all this unworthy sensitiveness on her own account, and give her a keener sense of Thy Pure Love!

I thank God that we have found out the mischief; discovery is half the cure. Do not be fidgetty; be simple and lowly.

XLIX.

"I SEE ANOTHER LAW . . . . WARRING AGAINST THE LAW OF MY MIND."

Oisy, *April* 6, 1702.

. . . I NEEDED your second letter to explain the first. No one could be more sorry for you than I am, or better appreciate your state; but I am not surprised at the duality which I perceive in you. Each person speaks after her own fashion, and one of the two must give way—of that there can be no doubt. The mind and utterance of the rebellious half are not your real self; the other is the reality, who means what she thinks and says. You mean it even when you do not know it; and you neither mean nor believe all that rushes through the imagination of that other person, who is so positive as to all she feels or fancies. Nothing can give the clue to this mystery but experience of such interior troubles. I repeat it, I feel deeply for you; but I am in no wise doubtful as to what God is doing for you. I will answer for your intentions, and am confident as to the persistent faithfulness of your heart under all these apparent waywardnesses. . . . I intreat you to take your own share, and unite yourself to my petitions that God's work may prosper in you.

L.

SEPARATED FRIENDS MEET IN GOD.

CAMBRAI, *April* 17, 1702.

. . . So M. Bourdon does not venture to let you move. . . . This is a positive decision of God's Providence, and we can only accept it in calm adoration. . . . Never mistrust the faithful Friend Who will never fail us, often as we fail Him. I will take for granted every conceivable act of faithlessness on your part;—well, what then? If you have been wanting towards God, all you have to do is to resist Him no longer. He is not like men, whose hollow selfishness turns to unchangeable indignation and wrath. Even if you have disappointed God hundreds of times, return sincerely to Him, cease to resist Him, and He will at once open His Arms to you. It is He Himself Who has prevented you by His Mercy, Who has inspired you with the wish to return. How can He fail to welcome the aspiration which He Himself has kindled in your heart?

"Wherefore do ye fear, O soul of little faith?" You will, it is true, be alone for some five or six weeks; but is it to be alone when you are with God? When He has joined us to one of His creatures, and subjects us to the conditions of such an union, we must cleave thereto, not for what we expect of man, but out of pure fidelity to God, Who is pleased to make use of that instrument. But all depends on not resisting the order of His Providence, but obeying it humbly. Wish what He wills, leave off any inward resistance, and all is done. God does not need our bodily presence to the fruition of unions He has formed,—our will is sufficient. Such union is maintained, although the sea separates us;—we meet familiarly in His Bosom Who knows neither time nor space, and Whose Immensity obliterates distance. We can communicate, understand, exchange intercourse and consolation, without seeing or hearing; God delights to supplement all. But if people are thrown together without such correspondence of heart, without being united through God, they are disturbed, excited, spent, dried up; for all peace leaves a heart which resists God. If such persons are a thousand miles apart, without hope of meeting or hearing from each other, they have no common ground in God, and nothing annihilates distance save the union of wills in Him. It is in Him as a Centre that we find each other, and that is so near a presence that tangible meeting is nothing as compared to it. Such intercourse is quite unlike that of conversation; not unfrequently souls thus knit together meet without being able to talk; they seem too near for words, too full of their common interest for external demonstrations. They are as one in God, and He is as one soul in their two separate bodies.

Remain peacefully, then, where God detains you, and when He summons you thence, go forth with your whole heart. Peace depends upon an unresisting will. Resume your former studies; renew your intercourse with your favourite and admirable friend S. Francis de Sales. Treat yourself like a convalescent who needs to be fed with dainties, and with but little at a time; it is a sort of infancy. Reading will gradually lead on to meditation, and that will expand your heart, and bring back your freedom with the Bridegroom. Let God work His Own Way, and join yourself to my intentions. Wherever I go I shall offer you to God, and you will be present with me in Him. How I long to see you again; but I am not impatient! God be with you.

LI.

PERSEVERANCE.

VEZON, *May* 13, 1702.

... ONE day of perseverance under trouble is more acceptable to God, and does more for the soul's progress, than many years spent in the intoxication of spiritual sweetness, in which we say like S. Peter, "It is good for us to be here."[1] Your friend needs you, and you see that you are helping her. . . . But while you are doing good to others, be sure you do not harm yourself. Give no heed to your own voice, hearken only to Him Who at once destroys and gives life. Above all, mistrust your fastidiousness, which is a most dangerous temptation. May God be in you, and fill you, so that there shall be no room for yourself.

LII.

NOT TO FOSTER SCRUPLES.

SAINT-GHISLAIN, *May* 19, 1702.

YOUR over warmth, Madame, really only consists in your fear of having been too warm. Never be afraid, I beg, of being too free with me. When I perceive any excess, I shall not wait for you to question me, I shall tell you very freely. As to your confessions, do as little that is wrong as you can till I return. I cannot give you any precise rule, for any rule runs a chance of feeding constraint and scruple with you. All must depend upon your confessor. Certainly the less often you go to confession the better.

[1] Matt. xvii. 4.

LIII.

OF SOME SOCIAL PERILS.

CAMBRAI, *June* 23, 1702.

I AM very sorry for your trouble. The things with which you reproach yourself are a mere nothing; it is not God's Spirit, but your fancy which recalls them. God never excites these self-consuming retrospections. Even when He points out our faults, He does it gently, condemning and comforting us simultaneously. He humbles without crushing, and makes us take His part against ourselves, so that in spite of shame at our weakness we are thoroughly at peace. "The Lord is not in the earthquake."[1] I will suppose that your love of conversation led you away somewhat, that you gave too much liberty to your wit, that self-conceit overpowered you; in short, I will suppose whatever your keen and exaggerated sensitiveness imagines. What then? Are you to renounce all society? can you close your door to your best friends who need you, to those whom you yourself know set forward your own nearness to God! Would you reject all those consolations without which you cannot reasonably hope restoration of health to your feeble, depressed system? Do you want to put an end

[1] 1 Kings xix. 11.

to yourself by a solitary life which would undermine your constitution, and leave you helpless? It is told of S. Bernard that once, while preaching with great success, he felt the flutterings of self-complacency within him, and was on the point of leaving the pulpit. But the Spirit of God gave him to understand that it was a subtle temptation, a scruple which thus alarmed him, and he pursued his sermon, saying to himself, "It was not vanity which brought me hither, and in spite of its flattery it shall not drive me hence."

Even if you committed real faults in this intercourse you could not give it up. It is not a question of great or mortal sin, but only of those venial sins which self-love is for ever renewing, and which we can never wholly avoid in this life. The occasions you would give up are providentially ordered as a necessary part of your calling in life; by cutting them off you would make yourself responsible for the faults of others, and for your own spiritual injury; you would close and wither your own heart.

Moreover, after such conversations do not fancy that God is punishing you by withdrawing from you, or depriving you of the spirit of prayer. On the contrary, it is merely your own scruples which disturb you and engross your attention with your imagined faults, thus making you resist the movements of simplicity and peace, leading you away from God's Presence, and stopping your inward supplies of grace. Do not listen to these useless scruples; try to be calm, learn to ignore whatever is unworthy to distract you from God. Never give way to any regret over such faults, save that which a quiet abiding in God's Presence may rouse in you. You will soon learn that all that loss of sweetness in prayer comes, not from God, but from your self-consuming habit of resisting His Spirit of Grace.

LIV.

SELF-DECEIT

Nov. 10, 1702.

THERE are two things which do you an infinity of harm. One is the tendency to scruples, rooted in your heart from childhood, and driven to an extreme point for so many years; the other is your persistency in always attempting to see and realise the good you do. Scruples often deprive you of all comfort and consciousness of love, by reason of the agitation they produce; while on the other hand the loss of that consciousness redoubles your scruples, for you fancy you are doing nothing, that you have lost God, and are under illusion, the moment you do not feel the conscious warmth of love. These two things ought to convince you of the extent of your self-love.

You have spent all your life in the belief that you are wholly devoted to others, and never self-seeking. Nothing so feeds self-conceit as this sort of internal testimony that one is quite free from self-love, and always generously devoted to one's neighbours. But all this devotion which seems to be for others is really to yourself. Your self-love reaches the point of perpetual self-congratulation that you are free from it; all your sensitiveness is lest you might not be fully satisfied with self: this is at the root of all your scruples. You may prove it by your indifference to the faults of others: if you thought of nothing save God and His Glory, you would be as keen and sensitive to others' losses as to your own. But it is the "I" which makes you so keen and sensitive. You want God as well as man to be always satisfied with you, and you want to be satisfied with yourself in all your dealings with God.

Besides, you are not accustomed to be content with a simple good-will—your self-love wants a lively emotion, a reassuring pleasure, some kind of charm or excitement. You are too much used to be guided by imagination, and to suppose that your mind and will are inactive unless you are conscious of their workings. And thus you are dependent upon a kind of excitement similar to that which the passions arouse, or theatrical representations. By dint of refinement you fall into the opposite extreme—a real coarseness of imagination. Nothing is more opposed, not only to the life of faith, but also to true wisdom. There is no more dangerous opening to illusion than the fancies by which people try to avoid illusion. It is imagination which leads us astray; and the certainty which we seek through imagination, feeling, and taste, is one of the most dangerous sources whence fanaticism springs. . . . This is the gulf of vanity and corruption which God would make you discover in your heart; you must look upon it with the calm and simplicity belonging to true humility. It is mere self-love to be inconsolable at seeing one's own imperfections; but to stand face to face with them, neither flattering nor tolerating them, seeking to correct one's self without becoming pettish,—this is to desire what is good for its own sake, and for God's, rather than merely treating it as a self-satisfying decoration.

So pray turn your scruples upon this useless search after self-satisfaction in doing right.

. . . Ought you to be so sensitive, even if I had formed an unjust opinion of you? Many holy souls have submitted to be unjustly condemned by prejudiced directors; why are you so alive to a far slighter prejudice, which, moreover, I altogether deny? . . . Mistrust your imagination and your intellect: I shall pray continually for you.

LV.

ON THE PRIVATION OF SENSIBLE SWEETNESS.

Cambrai, July 30, 1703.

It is long since anything has pleased me more than your letter of yesterday. . . . You must accustom yourself to privation: the great trouble it causes shows how much it is needed. It is only because we appropriate light, sweetness, and enjoyment, that it is so necessary that we should be stripped of all these things. So long as the soul clings to any consolation, it needs to be stripped thereof. Undoubtedly the God we feel to be beneficent and indulgent is still God, but it is God with His Gifts: God surrounded with darkness, privation, and desolation is God only. When a mother wants to attract her little one, she comes to him, her hands full of toys and sugarplums; but the father approaches his grown-up son without any presents. God goes still further; He veils His Face, He hides His Presence, and often only visits those He seeks to perfect through the utter darkness of simple faith. You are like a baby crying because you have missed your bonbons: God gives them to you now and then, and these ups and downs comfort the soul when it begins to be discouraged, while accustoming it at the same time to privation.

God does not intend either to spoil or discourage you; give yourself up then to these vicissitudes which so upset your soul, which, however, by accustoming it to have no abiding condition, make it supple and plastic to receive whatever impression God wills. It is so to say a heart-foundry: by dint of melting all the outlines of self are lost. Pure water has neither colour or form, it always takes the form and colour of the vessel containing it. Let this be your case with God.

As to painful or humiliating thoughts, whether concerning your faults or your temporal affairs, treat them as the sensitiveness of self-love: our pain at all these things is more humiliating than the things themselves. Put all together, the trouble and your perplexity at it, and carry the cross without trying to alter it one way or another. Directly that you bear it thus, in simple trust of God, you will be at rest, and your cross will become light.

LVI.

THE STRUGGLES OF SELF-WILL.

Aug. 23, 1703.

You see, my dear daughter, that all your troubles come from jealousy, or the sensitive self-love, or from some deep-down scruple which is closely allied to self-love.

And such troubles always carry disturbance with them. Both cause and effect prove that they are real temptations. The Spirit of God never inspires us with self-conceit; and so far from creating disturbance, it always fills the heart with peace. What could be a more certain proof of temptation than to see you in a kind of despair, rebelling against everything which God gives to lead you to Himself? Such rebellion is not natural, but God suffers temptation to drive you to such an extremity in order that you may more easily recognise that it is temptation. In the same way He suffers you to fall into certain faults in the presence of others, which are altogether contrary to your excessive delicacy and discretion, in order to mortify that delicacy and discretion which you cherish so jealously. He causes the ground to give under you, in order that you may not find any conscious stay either in yourself or your neighbour; and further, He suffers you to fancy that your neighbour judges you quite other than he really does, in order that your self-conceit may lose any flattering prop in that direction. The remedy is severe, but it needed nothing less to free you from yourself, and to force the entrenchment of your pride. You want to die, but to die without any pain, and in full health. You want to be tried, but only while looking on with conscious superiority at the trial. It is a saying of the old lawyers with respect to donations,

"Donner et retenir ne vaut," *i.e.* you cannot give and hold. You must give all or nothing when God asks it. If you have not courage to give, at least let Him take.

LVII.

THE CROSS EVERYWHERE.

Sept. 23, 1703.

... THE cross is everywhere. I can taste nothing save bitterness; but we must bear the heaviest cross quietly, and not only carry or drag it, but abide crushed and buried beneath it. I hope that God will spare you sufficiently to give you material for suffering—that is our daily bread. God only knows the right proportion, and we must live by faith in order to believe without seeing that God adapts our trials to our means of succour with an absolute and merciful certainty. This life of faith is the deepest of all death to self.

LVIII.

A NEW YEAR'S WISH.

Jan. 1, 1704.

How heartily I wish you a happy new year, in all simplicity and truth! Feeling does not depend upon ourselves—only will; and even our will cannot be measured: we cannot take it up like a glove and say, Here it is. You love your son without perpetually worrying yourself to *feel* your love, as you worry yourself to feel your love of God. It is enough that we will to love, and act as best we can accordingly in the spirit of such love. God has no touchy sensitiveness as we have. Let us go straight to Him, and that will do.

LIX.

ON BEING KEPT BACK FROM A SERMON.

Feb. 10, 1704.

A SUBMISSIVE will which yields to others is better than any number of sermons! It was doubtless out of exceeding care for your health, or some other good reason, that M. de Montberon refused you this little indulgence,—it is a mere trifle. You must adapt yourself to his wishes, and a sermon is but a small thing to sacrifice to them. He is one of the kindest men I know. The sermon was not suitable to you, and you may be consoled for not having heard it. A few words spoken after long silence by your own fireside are worth far more. Do enlarge your poor heart; God is ill at ease in straitened hearts. True love is too simple to be straitened. "Where the Spirit of the Lord is there is liberty."[1]

[1] 2 Cor. iii. 17.

LX.

THE DANGER OF SELF-CHOSEN PLANS.

March 24, 1712.

RESUME prayer and communion, my daughter, at whatever cost. You have withered your heart by so eagerly pressing your own wishes regardless of God's Will: this is the cause of all you are suffering. You have spent a great deal of time in making plans which were mere cobwebs, and a breath of wind has blown them away. You withdrew gradually 'from God, and He has withdrawn from you. You must return to Him, and give yourself up unreservedly to Him: there is no other way by which you can regain peace. Let go all your plans; God will do as He pleases with them. Even if they were to succeed through earthly means, He would not bless them. But if you offer them unreservedly to Him, He will turn everything to His Own merciful purposes, whether He does what you wish or not. The important thing is to resume meditation and prayer, whatever dryness, distraction, or weariness you may find in it. You deserve to be rejected of God after having rejected Him for the creature so long,—your patience will win Him again. But meanwhile persevere in your communions to strengthen your weakness. The weak need to be fed above all with bread. Do not argue, or give heed to your fancies, but communicate as soon as you can. . . . As to your friend, do not cut him off, but only see him in moderation. You will do him great injury, and a world of harm to yourself, if you do not observe such moderation. Tell him the truth gently as occasion offers. Speak only in a spirit of grace and self-abnegation; and as to the rest, do not adhere to your fancies about an absolute separation. We will talk all this over when I see you next.

LXI.

TO THE MARQUISE DE RISBOURG. ON SELF-SEEKING IN FRIENDSHIP.

April 24, 1712.

You are but seeking self, my dear daughter, in your search after human friendship, but you will not find what you look for. Your sensitiveness in friendship is only a refined self-love, but other people have self-love as well as you: everybody wants it all his own way! Moreover, you will never find peace or comfort in a selfish greediness of love; it will bear nought save thorns and prickles. What else do you deserve, when Infinite Goodness does not suffice you, and you do not feel God to be enough, without the addition of utterly frivolous amusements. Try to recover your recollection, and that without delay. Prayer must be your penance, until it once more becomes your nourishment.

LXII.

ON SLACKNESS IN RELIGIOUS LIFE.

April 13, 1713.

I CAN find no words better suited to you, my dear child, than those of S. John to the Bishop of Ephesus (supposed to be S. Timothy): "I have somewhat against thee, because thou hast left thy first love. Remember therefore from whence thou art fallen, and repent, and do the first works; or else I will come unto thee quickly, and will remove thy candlestick out of his place."[1] It is thus that God's Holy Spirit loves men without flattering them. He loves, yet threatens, but His very threats are love. He holds forth a penalty, so that men may not force Him to inflict it.

See how easily the best people fall gradually away without noticing it. Here is Timothy, whom S. Paul addresses as a "man of God,"[2] the angel of one of the holiest Churches of the East in those early days of religious prosperity; yet this angel falls, he "leaves his first love," his recollection, his prayer, his good works; he grows lax and careless. At first he does not perceive

[1] Rev. ii. 4, 5.   [2] 1 Tim. vi. 11.

his wanderings or his fall. He says to himself, "What harm am I doing? Is not my conduct upright and regular in the world's eyes? Must one not have some pleasure? it is scarce worth living without anything to cheer and amuse one!" It is thus that people ingeniously deceive themselves, and disguise their backsliding. But the Holy Spirit bids them hasten to open their eyes, and see "from whence they are fallen."

How far you are below your former standard! Remember the fervency of your prayers, your love of solitude, your jealous watch over recollection, and the strictness with which you shunned whatever could interfere with it. If you do not remember, others have not forgotten, and do not fail to ask, "What has become of all that fervour? There is nothing to be seen now but the love of amusement and pleasure, and restless *ennui* when there is a pause in these. It is not the same person. Can she be by way of being devout?"

Thus people fall by insensible degrees, and under fair pretences, from a state of sincere self-denial into a laxity which revives all the worst forms of selfishness. At least you should try to "remember whence you are fallen," and mourn over that "first love" which fostered you. You must try to resume those "first works" which you have exchanged in such a slothful way for mere vanities. You must gaze from afar on the desert in which you dwelt at peace with the True Comforter. You must say with the Prodigal Son, "I will arise and go to my Father, and will say unto Him, Father, I have sinned against Heaven and against Thee, and am no more worthy to be called Thy son." If at first He seems cold or hard, accept it humbly as a penance of which you stand greatly in need. If you fail in returning speedily to His Fatherly Breast, you hear what He would do: "I will come unto thee quickly, and will remove thy candlestick out of its place." He would take away the light which you do not use, and leave you in darkness; He would transfer His Precious Gifts which you have trodden under foot to some truer, more obedient, more faithful soul. You must resume your reading, your meditations, your silence, your former simplicity and lowliness.

LXIII.

TO A LADY.[1] HEARKENING TO GOD.

You let your taste and imagination have too much play. Strive to hearken more to God in meditation, and less to yourself. Self-conceit has less to say when it finds that it is not hearkened to. God's utterances to the soul are simple, calm, sustaining, even when they seem over-

[1] The following letters, to No. LXX., are written to the same person.

whelming; but self always speaks with an uncertain, disturbed, excited tone, even when its words are soothing. He who listens to God without making any plans for himself is really renouncing his own will.

LXIV.

HOW TO MEET SICKNESS.

Do not be disturbed because of your malady; you are in God's Hands. The thing is to live as if you expected daily to die; then everything will be ready, since preparation for death consists in detachment from the world, and attachment to God. While you are so feeble, do not let yourself be fretted about the regularity of your meditation. Exactitude and exertion of the brain may hurt your weak health. It is enough in your languid state if you renew the Presence of God quietly as often as you find that you are forgetting it. A natural, familiar intercourse with God, in which you tell Him all your troubles in full confidence, and in which you ask Him to help you, will not exhaust, while it will nourish your spiritual life.

LXV.

ON GIVING WAY TO THE IMAGINATION.

I THINK you ought to abstain wholly from your imaginary dialogues. Although some may tend to kindle pious feelings, I think it is a dangerous habit for you. From such as those you will unconsciously pass on to others, which will foster your excitement, or encourage your love of the world. Better far suppress them all, I do not mean that you should stop them forcibly,—you might as well try to stop a torrent; enough if you do not voluntarily harbour them. When you perceive that your imagination is beginning to work, be satisfied with turning to God, without directly combatting these fancies. Let them drop, occupying yourself in some useful way. If it be a time of meditation or prayer, treat all such idle thoughts as distractions, and return quietly to God as soon as you are conscious of them, but do so without anxiety, scruples, or agitation. If, on the other hand, such imaginations trouble you when engaged in external work, the work will help you to resist such castle building. It would even be well at first to find some companion, or to set about some difficult task, with a view to breaking the thread of such thoughts, and getting rid of the habit.

LXVI.

THE SAME SUBJECT.

You must positively suppress this trifling of the imagination, it is pure waste of time, a very dangerous occupation, and a temptation voluntarily incurred. It is a duty never to yield to it voluntarily. Perhaps, owing to habit, your imagination will still beset you with fancies in spite of yourself; but at all events do not yield to them, and try quietly to get rid of them whenever you become aware that they are occupying you. The best means of getting rid of them is to occupy yourself in meditation, or in some active work if meditation does not quiet your excited imagination.

LXVII.

ON MEDITATION.

It is well always to place some simple, solid, practical subject before your mind in meditation. If you do not find matter for it in such a subject, but are rather drawn to general union with God, keep to that as long as you feel so drawn; but do not make a habit of it: always be stedfast in taking a subject, and try to occupy and feed your mind with it. Accept freely all lights and emotions which are given you in meditation, but do not trust to any of those things which may flatter your vanity and fill you with idle self-complacency.

It is better to be very humble and ashamed of the faults one has committed, than satisfied with one's meditation, and puffed up with a notion that one is very advanced, because one has had a flow of fine feelings and aspirations in prayer. Accept whatever may come from God's helping Hands, but be sure that these gifts will turn to most dangerous illusions if you drop into self-complacency through their means.

The great thing is to mortify self, to obey God, to mistrust self, to bear the Cross. All the same I am very glad that you can meditate now without that forced effort which hampered you so greatly. Your meditation is calmer, and you are more helpful to your neighbours, but you must take care that this holy freedom never turns to laxity or dissipation.

LXVIII.

THE VALUE OF PRIVATIONS.

I AM truly sorry for the *contre-temps* which have hindered my seeing you; meanwhile strive diligently to follow the light God gives you with a view to mortifying your self-consciousness and sensitiveness. Those who give themselves up entirely to God's designs are as ready to be deprived of consolations as to enjoy them; indeed often a privation which humbles and upsets our own plans is more useful than the greatest plenty of sensible sweetness.

If it is often very wholesome to be deprived of the conscious Presence of God and His Comfort, why may it not be very good for you to be deprived of my presence and my poor counsels? God is ever near, even when He seems afar off from us, provided we bear His seeming absence in a spirit of love to Him, and self-mortification. Accustom yourself to bear some weariness. Children, as they grow, learn to give up their mother's milk, to walk alone, and to eat dry bread.

LXIX.

HOW TO USE EAGER ASPIRATIONS.

I AM well pleased with your condition,—you are quite right to tell me what you think in all truthfulness. Do not hesitate to write and tell me what you believe God requires of you.

It is not to be wondered at that you should have a sort of jealous eagerness and ambition to advance in the spiritual life, and to be in the confidence of noteworthy servants of God. Self-love naturally seeks successes of this kind, which are flattering to it. But the real thing that matters is, not to satisfy your ambition by some brilliant advance in virtue, or by being taken into the confidence of distinguished persons, but to mortify the flattering tendencies of self-love, to humble yourself, to love obscurity and contempt, and to seek God only.

People cannot become perfect by dint of hearing or reading about perfection. The chief thing is not to listen to yourself, but silently to give ear to God; to renounce all vanity, and apply yourself to real virtue. Talk little, and do much, without caring to be seen. God will teach you more than all the most experienced persons or the most spiritual books can do. What is it you want so much to know? What do you need to learn, save to be poor in spirit and to find all wisdom in Christ crucified. "Knowledge puffeth up;" it is only "charity which edifies."[1] Do you be content to aim at charity. Do you need any such great knowledge in order to love God and deny yourself for His love? You already know a great deal more than you practise. You do not need the acquirement of fresh knowledge half so much as to put in practice that which you already possess. How people delude themselves, when they expect to advance by means of argument and inquisitive-

[1] 1 Cor. viii. 1.

ness! Be lowly, and never expect to find gifts which are God's only in man.

LXX.

TO A LADY LIVING IN THE WORLD.[1] ON THE DESIRE FOR KNOWLEDGE.

LIVE quietly from day to day, Mademoiselle, without thinking about the future. Perhaps there may not be a future for you. Even the present is not really yours, and you must only use it as is consistent with the Will of God, to Whom it actually belongs. Go on with the exterior works you have in hand, since you find them easy and attractive; keep your rule diligently, in order to avoid dissipation and the consequences of your exceeding liveliness. Above all, use each present moment faithfully,—that will bring you all needful grace.

It is not enough to practise detachment, you must become small in your own conceits.[2] By detachment we only renounce external things; by this lowering our mental stature we renounce self. By it we renounce all lofty aims. There is a lofty aim after knowledge and good-

---

[1] This lady appears to have been subject to the restraint of living in the house of an aged relative; and ultimately to have joined a community. The letters are not dated.

[2] Fénelon's word,—a very favourite one with him, is "*s'apetisser:*" we have no English word precisely corresponding, but it bears the same meaning as that of S. John iii. 30, "He must increase, but I must *decrease.*"

ness which may be more dangerous than the loftiest of worldly fortune, because it is less overt. We need to be lowly in all things, not reckoning on anything of our own, least of all on our own courage and virtue. You reckon overmuch upon your courage, your disinterested uprightness. A child has nothing really its own, no power of discrimination,—it treats a diamond as it would an apple. Do you be like a child. Count nothing as yours. Forget yourself. Yield on all sides; let the least be greater than you.

Pray with your whole heart, with simplicity, out of pure affection, not with your intellect, like a person holding an argument.

The real learning you need is stripping off self, thorough recollection, silence of heart before God, renunciation of intellect, a taste for lowliness, obscurity, helplessness, and unimportance. This is an ignorance which alone can teach all the truths which no knowledge can impart, or at least most superficially.

LXXI.

DANGERS OF HUMAN APPLAUSE.

M.'s good health and your present tranquillity rejoice me. Nevertheless I am somewhat fearful lest self-love may too keenly relish this ease, so different to the discomfort you have experienced. Contradiction and other humiliating circumstances are far more profitable than success. You know that your troubles made you find out what you never knew before about yourself; and I am afraid lest the authority, the success and admiration which are easily acquired among second class people in the country, should foster your imperious temper, and make you self-satisfied as you were before. Such self-satisfaction will mar the best ordered life, because it is incompatible with humility.

We can only be humble so long as we give heed to all our own infirmities. The consciousness of these should be predominant; the soul should feel burdened by them, groan under them, and that groaning should be as a perpetual prayer to be set free from "the bondage of corruption," and admitted into the "glorious liberty of the children of God:" overwhelmed by its own faults, the soul should look for no deliverance save from the great Mercy of Jesus Christ. Woe to the soul which is self-satisfied, which treats God's Gifts as its own merits, and forgets what is due to Him!

Your remedy for dissipation and dryness will be to set apart regular seasons for reading and prayer; only to mix yourself up in outward matters when it is really necessary; and to attend more to softening the harshness of your judgment, to restraining your temper, and humbling your mind, than to upholding your opinion even when it is right; and finally, to humble yourself, whenever you find that an undue warmth concerning the affairs of others has led you to forget the one all-important matter to yourself, Eternity. "Learn of Me," Jesus Christ says to you; "for I am meek and lowly of heart: and ye shall find rest unto your souls."[1] Be sure that grace, inward peace, and the Blessing of the Holy Spirit will be with you, if you can maintain a gentle humility amid all your external perplexities.

LXXII.

HOW TO BEAR AFFRONTS.

I AM touched by your troubles, but I can only pity you, and ask God to comfort you. You greatly need that He should impart His Holy Spirit to guide you in your difficulties, and to moderate your natural vehemence under circumstances so calculated to excite it. As to . . . I think you should speak of that to none save God in prayer on behalf of the person who insulted you. I have often fancied that I saw you to be very sensitive on that point; and God always touches us in our weak place. Men are not killed by a blow on the extremities—the nails or hair,—but by an injury to the vital parts, which

[1] Matt. xi. 29.

are called noble. When God purposes to make us die to self, He always touches that which is the very essence of our life,—He adapts our cross to each. Let yourself be humbled; calm and silence under humiliation are a great benefit to the soul. One is sometimes tempted to talk humility, and it is easy to find plenty of opportunities for so doing, but it is better to be humbly silent. Talkative humility is always suspicious; talk is a certain relief to self-conceit.

Do not get angry about what people say; let them talk while you try to do God's Will. As to the will of men, you could never come to an end of satisfying it, nor is it worth the trouble. Silence, peace, and union with God ought to comfort you under whatever men may falsely say. You must be friendly to them, without counting on their friendship. They come and go; let them go,—they are but as chaff scattered by the wind. Only see God's Hand in what they do; He alone wounds or comforts us through their means. You need all your resolution in your present position, but at the same time your quickness of temper requires checks and impediments. Possess your soul in patience. Frequently recall the Presence of God, so as to calm yourself, to humble and adapt yourself to the little ones. Nothing is really great save lowliness, charity, mistrust of self, detachment from one's own opinion and will.

All stiff, harsh goodness is contrary to Jesus Christ: God knows how truly I am yours in Him.

LXXIII.

RECOLLECTION IN A LIFE OF RESTRAINT.

I CAN say no more to you than what I have always said: simply obey your director, without heeding your own likings or opinions. You are fortunate in the guidance of a very pious and enlightened man. For myself, I can only say generally, that you ought, I think, to persevere in setting aside seasons of recollection, otherwise you will become a cross to her whose support you are called to be. You have a terrible inclination for dissipation and foolish complaisance; you like to praise and be praised; you are conscious of a vigour in your intellect and your natural powers which fosters pride. Nothing but recollection can mortify this life of pride, and moderate your intolerable vehemence.

There are two things to be heeded as to your hours of recollection; first, you must never reserve them out of a spirit of contradiction or impatience with M. . . . who is disposed to engross you. Whenever you feel that you are actuated by this unworthy spirit, punish yourself by yielding to her for that day. The other rule is only to set aside such time as is necessary in order to recollect and strengthen your soul; let there be nothing for your own private amusement, or for mere curiosity, which is a great snare to you. And while reserving such time steadily, it should be done quietly and gently.

Let your reading and meditation be simple, less to satisfy your intellect than your heart. Whatever seems to fill the one is merely puffing up; you think to quicken zeal, while really you are quickening pride. It is not a question of much knowledge, but of knowing how to abase yourself and to be as a little child in God's Hand.

As to topics which excite fear, I do not think you need force yourself to approach them. You will often meet very worthy people who urge you to do so, and who tremble themselves because they do not see you tremble; but do not be troubled; follow your own leading quietly, and so long as you are stedfast in recollection and humility be at rest. The fear of offending God is fear enough.

As to a curious spirit even about good books you should repress it; you have found by experience that it harms you, and you should be grateful to God for having taught you this. Under a pretence of seeking information people often foster tastes which feed their self-conceit, and keep up a mental pride very contrary to the Spirit of God. It is by a childlike spirit that you will gain true knowledge, which is that of the heart, not the knowledge which merely dazzles us from without.

LXXIV.

PATIENCE UNDER CONTRADICTION.

A HEATED imagination, vehement feeling, a world of argument, and flow of words, are really useless. The practical thing is to act in a spirit of detachment, doing what one can by God's Light, and being content with such success as He gives. Such continuous death to self is a blessed life which but few realise. A single word quietly spoken under such influences will go further, even in worldly matters, than the most eager, bustling exertions. It is the Spirit of God speaking with His Own strength and authority. He enlightens, persuades, touches, edifies. Scarcely anything has been said, but everything has been done. On the contrary, when people let loose their natural excitability, they talk interminably, indulge endless, subtle, superfluous imaginations; they are afraid of not saying and doing enough,—they get warm, excited,—they exhaust themselves without anything being the better for it. Your disposition greatly needs such warnings; they are hardly less requisite for your body's sake than for that of your soul; and your doctor and director would be of one mind in this matter.

Let the river flow beneath its bridges; let men be men, that is to say, weak, vain, inconstant, unjust, false, presumptuous. Let the world be the world, in short; and verily you cannot hinder it. Let everybody follow their natural disposition and habits; you cannot remould them, it is easier to let them alone and bear with them. Accustom yourself to put up with unreasonableness and injustice. Abide tranquilly in God's Bosom; He sees all these evils more clearly than you do, yet He suffers them. Be content with doing what little depends upon you well, and let all else be as though it were not. I am very glad to hear that you have some hours set apart: use them neither as a miser nor a prodigal.

LXXV.

BENEFITS OF LOOKING DEATH IN THE FACE.

It is a good thing to go down to the gates of death; we see God more closely there, we get accustomed to what must come ere long. One should surely gain self-knowledge by drawing so near to God's Judgment and His Eternal Truth. How great, how all in all He seems; we do indeed bow powerless when we approach Him so closely, and the veil which hides Him is all but lifted! Use this grace for your greater detachment from the world, and still more from yourself; for we cleave to all outer things for the sake of self, and all other attachments can be traced to that as their ultimate source. Love God, and renounce self for love of Him; do not cling to your own talents or strength; indulge no self-complacency in His Gifts, such as disinterestedness, equity, sincerity, generosity towards others. All these come from God, but they all turn to poison, and simply puff us up directly that we put our secret trust in them. We need to be as nothing in our own eyes, and always to act accordingly; all our lives we need to be hidden, and as it were annihilated, as our Dear Lord hides Himself in the Sacrament of His Love.

LXXVI.

THE NECESSITY AND BENEFIT OF SUFFERING.

I SYMPATHISE with all your sorrows, but we must carry the Cross of Jesus Christ during this brief life. The time for suffering will soon be past, and that for reigning with the God of Comfort, Who will wipe away every tear with His Own Hand, in Whose Presence all pain and groaning will vanish for ever, will shortly come. While this brief season of trial lasts let us beware of losing anything of the grace of the cross. Be it ours to suffer humbly and quietly. Self-love exaggerates our griefs, and enhances them in the imagination. A cross borne simply, without the ingenious additions of self-consciousness, is half lifted off us. Those who suffer with such loving simplicity are not only happy in spite of this cross, they are happy because of it; for love delights to suffer on behalf of the beloved, and the cross which likens them to their Beloved One is a bond of union which consoles them under its own weight.

Do you bear the heavy burden of a very aged person who can no longer bear her own. The mind becomes weak at so great an age; goodness itself, unless very deeply rooted, seems to grow slack; temper and restlessness acquire all the strength which the mind loses, and theirs is the only activity which remains. Surely this is a most precious cross for you! you must accept it, bear it daily. It involves a very absolute self-renunciation both mental and bodily. It is a great blessing, however, that you can have some hours of freedom in which to be at peace in the Dear Lord's Bosom. That is when you must refresh yourself, and gain new strength for your toils. Take care of your health, relieve your mind by intervals of cheerful relaxation and rest. As age advances, less and less must be expected of a person who has no resources;—you must expect little or nothing from her, neither must you expect too much of yourself.

LXXVII.

NEED OF CALMING NATURAL ACTIVITY.

I AM afraid lest your natural activity should consume you amid the irksome details with which you are surrounded. You cannot take too much pains to subdue your natural temperament by prayer, and by a frequent renewal of God's Presence through the day. A Christian who grows eager over worldly trifles, and who suddenly awakes to the sense of God's Presence amid such eagerness, is like a child whose mother catches him suddenly having lost his temper over a game; he is quite ashamed at being found out. Be it ours to abide tranquilly, fulfilling all outward duties as well, or as little amiss, as we can, while inwardly we are absorbed by Him Who is alone worthy of all our love. Whenever you become conscious of the impulses of your nature, throw them aside, so that grace may possess you wholly. It is well to stop directly that we find nature getting the upper hand. Such fidelity to grace is almost as beneficial to the body as to the soul,—there is no neglect, and yet none of Martha's trouble.

LXXVIII.

FORBEARANCE TO OTHERS.

I AM sorry for you, but you must bear on. We are sent into this world only to be purified by mortification of inclinations and self-will. Let self die in you then: you have first-rate opportunities,—it were a pity to lose them! I am as convinced as you are that the daily rule should not be infringed, but you must deal pitifully with the infirmities of others. You can recoup in detail what you lose in the gross. It requires some managemen to deal with fanciful people; if you show plainly all that you want to do you throw them into despair; while, on the other hand, if you give them the least hope of conquering you they will give you no peace until they get their own way. So you must learn at times to slip quietly over certain matters, while abiding absolutely firm as to what is essential.

But remember that real firmness is gentle, humble, and quiet. Anything like sharp, harsh, restless firmness is unworthy of God's work. We are told that Wisdom "sweetly ordereth all things:"[1] do you the like; and if ever you are betrayed into acting roughly, humble your-

---

[1] Wisd. viii. 1.

self without reserve. Confess that you are often in error as to manner, and in substance keep to your rule. In other respects you cannot be too obliging or too assiduous. There is no manner of reading or prayer which will teach you so much self-renunciation as this subjection, provided that in your more private hours you attain sufficient recollection to make good use thereof, and that the distraction of business does not harden your heart. In a word, make as great a point of recollection as possible, and give all the rest of your time to charity, which is never weary, which endures in all self-forgetfulness, and becomes as a little child for the love of others.

LXXIX.

TO ONE ENTERING THE RELIGIOUS LIFE.
ON CALMNESS OF MIND.

I PRAY that this new year may be a renewed season of grace and blessing to you. I am not surprised that you do not enjoy recollection as you did in first issuing from a prolonged state of distressing excitement. Everything gets exhausted in time. A naturally lively mind accustomed to activity is sure to languish directly that it is thrown into solitude and comparative indolence. For a great many years you have been inevitably forced into dissipation and external activity, and that made me in the long-run dread this quiet life for you. At first you were upheld by the novice's fervour, to which nothing is hard; you cried out with S. Peter, "It is good for us to be here." But the same Evangelist tells us that S. Peter "knew not what he said," and it is often so with us. In moments of fervour we fancy we can do all things; in counter moments of temptation and depression we think we can do nothing, and that all is lost. In both alike we are mistaken.

The wandering imagination which tries you ought to be no matter of surprise. You brought the elements thereof with you, even when you were so keen after recollection. Natural disposition, habits of life, everything in you tends to activity and energy,—it was merely weariness and exhaustion which made a different manner of life attractive to you. But gradually, by faithful corresponding to grace, you will really enter into that life of concentration into which heretofore you have had a mere passing glimpse. God often gives it in first beginnings, to show His children whither He is leading them; and then He withdraws it, to teach us that it is not our own; that we have no power to acquire it of ourselves, or to retain it; that, in short, it is a gift of grace, which we must seek in all humility.

Do not be alarmed because you find yourself quick,

impatient, imperious, decided; such is your natural character,—you must feel it. As S. Augustine says, we must bear the yoke of daily shame for our sins. We must feel our weakness, our misery, our own powerlessness to correct what is amiss. We must have no hope in ourself, and hope only in God. We must bear with self without flattery, and without neglecting the means necessary to correct it. While waiting for God to deliver us from self, we need to know it thoroughly. Let us humble ourselves beneath His All-Powerful Hand; let us be supple and plastic, yielding to Him directly that we feel the assertions of self-love. Be silent as much as is possible; avoid hasty decisions; withhold your opinions, your likes and dislikes. Pause and break off your activity whenever you become conscious of its excess, and do not let yourself go headlong after your warm feelings even when lawful.

LXXX.

ALL FOR GOD.

WHAT I most desire for you is a certain calmness, which recollection, detachment, and love of God alone can give. S. Augustine says that whatever we love outside God so much the less do we love Him; it is as a brook whence part of the waters is turned aside. Such a diversion takes away from that which is God's, and thence arise harass and trouble. God would have all, and His jealousy cannot endure a divided heart; the slightest affection apart from Him becomes a hindrance, and causes estrangement. The soul can only look to find peace in love without reserve.

Dissipation,[1] the great foe of recollection, excites all human feelings, distracts the soul, and drives it from its true resting-place. Further still, it kindles the senses and imagination; and to quiet them again is a hard task, while the very effort to do so is in itself an inevitable distraction.

Concern yourself as little as possible with external matters. Give a quiet, calm attention to those things assigned to your care by Providence at proper seasons, and be sure that you can accomplish a great deal more by quiet thoughtful work done as in God's Sight, than by all the busy eagerness and over-activity of your restless nature.

LXXXI.

HOW TO DO ALL IN THE SPIRIT OF PRAYER.

ALL you have to do is to turn your energies inwardly upon yourself. Do not be disheartened at your faults;

---

[1] The sense in which Fénelon uses this word must always be borne in mind, not that in modern use among ourselves, but "a scattering abroad," its original meaning.

bear with, while correcting yourself, as we try to bear with and correct those committed to our charge. Try to cast away that restless activity which exhausts you physically, and leads you into faults as well. Accustom yourself gradually to let your mental prayer spread over all your daily external occupations. Speak, act, work quietly, as though you were praying, as indeed you ought to be.

Do everything without excitement, simply in the spirit of grace. So soon as you perceive natural activity gliding in, recall yourself quietly into the Presence of God. Hearken to what the leadings of grace prompt, and say and do nothing but what God's Holy Spirit teaches. You will find yourself infinitely more quiet, your words will be fewer and more effectual, and while doing less what you do will be more profitable. It is not a question of a hopeless mental activity, but a question of acquiring a quietude and peace in which you readily advise with your Beloved as to all you have to do. Such consultation, simple and brief though it be, will be more easily held than the bustling, restless arguments we hold within ourselves when natural energy has its way.

When once the heart is steadily bent towards God, we easily learn to withhold the hasty action of nature, and to wait for the time when we can act under the impulse of God's Grace only. It is continual death unto self which quickens the life of faith. That death is a real life, because peace-giving grace takes the place of disturbing natural causes. I entreat you try to train yourself to such a cultivation of the inner spirit, and then gradually everything will become prayer in you. You will not be free from suffering, but a peaceful suffering is one half relieved.

LXXXII.

CARE OF HEALTH AND DUTY.

You must not heed your scruples as to the indulgences conceded by your community. Your constitution is very delicate; you are not young, and a trifle would upset you. Do not wait till you are ill to spare your strength. The wise course is to foresee evils, rather than wait till they come. It is not allowable to run any risks in your present condition. In spite of these little indulgences, your life will not be very voluptuous. Mentally you may practise greater mortification. You must stifle your restlessness, renounce your self-will, retrench inquisitiveness, your longing after success, and your eagerness to attract all that gratifies self-conceit. Silence, whereby to cultivate the Presence of God, is the best remedy for all our troubles; it is a very practicable mode of self mortification in the most ordinary life.

Utilise your rest for calming yourself, softening your temper, fostering charity, humbling presumption, checking impetuosity, cultivating recollection and the Presence of God, together with that gentleness and consideration which are due to your neighbour. "Do this and ye shall live." God has moulded your disposition so as to contain a great treasure, by giving you wherewithal to sacrifice and crush out self daily and hourly. Things which would scarcely rouse other people touch you to the very core. You can feel nothing by halves. But it is well that you should realise this, so as to be on your guard against your likes and dislikes.

LXXXIII.

OVER-EAGERNESS.

Do not give way to the quickness of your likes and dislikes, and mistrust that fervid zeal which lays you open to perilous mistakes. Do not be hasty about anything, especially about such a matter as a change of abode. Avoid dissipation, without exposing yourself to overmuch weariness and *ennui*. Do not be afraid of giving yourself the relief of a little really good Christian society; be content with such inward fervour as God gives you, without trying to force it up to some consciously higher mark. The great thing is to fulfil God's Will honestly in denying self, in spite of all the deadness and repugnance one may feel. I pray that our Lord may give you peace, not to feed your self-will and self-pleasing, but to lead you on in self-renunciation for His Sake

LXXXIV.

PATIENCE IN SPIRITUAL PRIVATION.

I AM always pleased to hear of you; and now you will be surprised, yet must forgive me for another source of satisfaction, which is to see you with somewhat less of that sensible fervour, on which I felt you were resting too much. It is a good thing to feel one's weakness, and to learn by experience that all such fervour is but temporary. While we have it, it is God's Compassion ministering to our weakness; it is the milk of babes; but as time goes on we must be weaned, and learn to eat the dry bread of a more advanced age.

If we always possessed such taste and readiness for recollection, we should be sorely tempted to reckon upon it as our own downright possession; we should not realise either our weakness or our proneness to evil; we should be deficient in mistrust of self, and not have sufficient recourse to prayer. But when this conscious fervour is liable to interruption, we know what we lose; we remember whence it comes; we are forced to humble ourselves and seek it from God; we serve Him all the more faithfully in that we find less delight in the service; we constrain ourselves; we sacrifice our tastes; we no longer sail with wind and stream, but by sheer strength against both; we attain full mastery over self; we may be in trouble and bitterness, but if so, we accept them, and do not cleave to God only because it is pleasant to do so; we are ready to accept pleasure only when God sends it; we acknowledge our weakness, and realise that it is out of indulgence that He does so send it; and when He takes it away we acquiesce readily, believing that He knows far better than we do what we need.

The one thing which always depends on ourselves is a conformable will, and this will is all the purer when it is bare and cold, yet stedfast. Be as regular in your fixed season for meditation as though it came quite easily to you. Make use of those times in the day when you are only partially occupied with external things, to occupy yourself inwardly with the things of God; for instance, while doing needlework you can maintain a close sense of the Presence of God. Such conscious sense of His Presence is most difficult during conversation, but even then you can frequently recall a general sense of it, overruling your every word, and repressing all that is over-eager, all savouring of pride or contempt, all sallies of self-conceit. Bear with yourself, but do not flatter yourself. Work diligently and consecutively, yet calmly and without self-conscious impatience, at the correction of your faults.

LXXXV.

IN SICKNESS AND TRIAL.

I HEAR that your health has been very much deranged, and I am somewhat alarmed. You know that sickness is a precious grace of God, given that we may realise our spiritual through our bodily weakness. We flattered ourselves that we held this life in contempt, and aspired only after the heavenly home; but when age and sickness bring the end near, self revives and takes fright; and then we find no real longing for the kingdom of Christ within us, nought save indolence and cowardice, lukewarmness, dissipation, a cleaving to everything we fancied we had renounced. Such a humiliating experience is often more useful than the most fervid feelings, on which we were disposed to rely overmuch. The great thing is to give ourselves up to the Spirit of Grace, and let Him loosen our hold on everything earthly.

Remember your exceeding delicacy, and accept all the indulgence which your kind and wise superior suggests; you must not run any risks with such shattered health. Recollection, quietness, obedience, offering up your life, patience in sickness, are quite enough in the way of mortification.

I sympathise fully with your grief. You have lost a very dear sister, who most thoroughly deserved your love; God has in her taken away one of your greatest comforts, but it is in the jealousy of His Love. Even in the purest, most lawful friendships, He sees the roots of self-love, which He wills to cut out to the last fibre. Leave Him to work His Will. Adore that severity which is all love, and strive to enter into His designs. Why should we weep for those who will never weep more, whose tears God has for ever wiped away? We are in fact only weeping for ourselves, and poor humanity may be excused some such self-compassion. But faith certifies us that we shall soon be reunited to those whom in our earthliness we call lost. Do you live by faith, regardless of flesh and blood. You will find her again in our common Centre, the Bosom of God. Take care of your health under this sharp trial; tranquillise your mind before God, and do not hesitate to solace yourself with the society of some congenial, pious friends. We ought not to be ashamed to deal with ourselves as children when it is needful.

LXXXVI.

LUKEWARMNESS.

WHAT a relief it would be only to see those who are really friends in God's Sight, and to be sheltered from all others! I could often sigh amid my many engagements after the freedom of solitude, but one must hold on one's way and work on without heeding inclination. Shun *ennui*, and let your natural activity find some outlet. See a few persons whose society is not exciting, but who bring you relaxation. One does not want a great deal of society, and it is well to learn not to be too fastidious, —enough if we can find some peaceable and tolerably reasonable people. You should read, work, walk when it is fine, and so vary your occupations as not to grow weary of any.

As to your lukewarmness and lack of conscious inward life, I am not surprised at this trial depressing you. Nothing is harder to bear. But it seems to me you have only two things to do, one of which is to avoid whatever excites and dissipates you, whereby you cut off the source of dangerous distractions, which dry up prayer. You cannot expect to find interior nourishment if you live only for what is exterior. Strict watchfulness in giving up whatever makes you too eager and impetuous in conversation is an absolute necessity if you would win the spirit of recollection and prayer. No one can have a relish for both God and the world simultaneously, and whatever spirit you have carried about with you through the day's occupations you will carry to your appointed hours of prayer.

Then, after retrenching whatever superfluities dissipate your mind, you must try very often to renew the Presence of God, even amid those occupations which are right and necessary, guarding against your self-will. Try continually to act by the leadings of grace and in the spirit of self-renunciation. By degrees you will come to it, by frequently checking the rapidity of your lively disposition, and hearkening to God's Voice within, and letting Him possess you wholly.

LXXXVII.

HOW TO BEAR WITH OTHERS.

... In order to be satisfied even with the best people, we need to be content with little, and to bear a great deal. Even the most perfect people have many imperfections, and we ourselves have no fewer. Our faults combined with theirs make mutual toleration a difficult matter, but we can only "fulfil the law of Christ" by "bearing one another's burdens."[1] There must be a

---

[1] Gal. vi. 2.

mutual, loving forbearance. Frequent silence, habitual recollection, prayer, self-detachment, giving up all critical tendencies, watchfulness to put aside all the idle imaginations of jealous, fastidious self-love,—all these will go far to maintain peace and unity. How many troubles we might save ourselves thereby! Happy he who neither gives ear to himself nor to the idle talk of others!

Be content to lead a quiet life where God has placed you. Be obedient, bear your little daily crosses,—you need them, and it is out of pure mercy God lays them on you. The great thing is thoroughly to despise yourself, and to be willing that others should despise you, if God so will. Feed wholly on Him. S. Augustine says that his mother lived only on prayer. Do you the like, and die to all else. But we can only live to God by continual dying to self.

LXXXVIII.

THE IMPRESSIONS CAUSED BY THE PROSPECT OF DEATH.

I AM nowise surprised to hear that death makes a livelier impression on you as age and infirmity gradually bring it nearer. I feel the same myself. There is a period when death forces itself oftener and more forcibly upon our thoughts than before. Moreover, in times of retirement one has fewer distractions to divert them from this weighty matter. God uses this sharp trial in order to disabuse us as to our own courage, to make us feel how weak we are, and keep us humble beneath His Hand.

Nothing can be more humbling than a disturbed imagination, which prevents our realising our wonted confidence in God. It is the very furnace of affliction, wherein the heart is purified by experience of its own weakness and worthlessness. "In Thy Sight shall no man living be justified;"[1] and again, "The heavens are not clean in His Sight;"[2] and assuredly "in many things we offend all."[3] We perceive our faults, we do not see our virtues; indeed it would be very dangerous for us to perceive them if they be veritable.

The thing to be done is to go on straight forward and unremittingly with this anxiety as we tried to go on in God's ways before we felt it. Should our anxiety bring to light anything needing correction, we ought to be faithful to that light, but with the help of some safe advice for fear of falling into scruples. Then we should abide in peace, not hearkening to self-love when it grows pathetic at the thought of death, but loosening our hold on life, offering it to God, and giving one's self up to Him trustfully. As S. Ambrose lay dying, those around asked him if he were not troubled with fear of God's

[1] Ps. cxliii. 2.   [2] Job xv. 15.   [3] James iii. 2.

judgments. He only answered, "We have a good Master." And this is what we should reply to ourselves. We must die surrounded by impenetrable uncertainty, not only as to God's judgments concerning us, but also as to our own real dispositions. It is needful, as S. Augustine says, that we be reduced to the point of having nothing to offer God save our misery and His Mercy. Our misery is the very cause of His Mercy, and that Mercy is our strength. When you are depressed, read whatever is best suited to foster trust, and to comfort your heart. "Truly God is loving unto Israel: even unto such as are of a clean heart."[1] Ask Him to give you that clean heart which He so greatly prizes, and which makes Him so compassionate to our infirmities.

LXXXIX.

TO A RELIGIOUS IN ILLNESS.

WE must learn to sit loose to life. Suffering and sickness are our apprenticeship for death. Let us cheerfully offer our brief, frail, troublesome life to God—it is service rendered to Him by the renunciation of what is really worthless.

Yield to the care bestowed on you by your superior and your community. Real simplicity lies in yielding

[1] Ps. lxxiii. 1.

to those set over us, after duly telling them one's own mind, and in doing what one would tell others similarly placed to do.

Be at peace in your solitude, without hearkening to the disputes of the day; be content to hearken to the Church without arguing. They are happy who are willing to be poor in spirit,—such inward poverty is our best treasure. Even the wisest know nothing unless they are content to be as babes. Tell God your anxieties for the Church's peace, but do not talk to men,—a humble, docile silence will be your strength. Bear patiently your cross of sickness. Your present vocation is to be silent, to obey, to suffer, to give yourself up to God for life or death,—this is your daily bread. It is hard and dry, but it is better than all else, and the most real sustenance of the life of faith, which is a continual self-denial.

XC.

ON DRYNESS IN DEVOTION.

I HAVE observed that you reckon rather overmuch upon your fervour and recollection: God has withdrawn these visible gifts to teach you detachment, that you may learn how weak you are of yourself, and to accustom you to serve Him without the conscious satisfaction which makes all service easy. We do Him a far more real service when the very same things are done without satisfaction and against the grain. It is a small service I render my friend, if, being fond of walking and possessing strong legs, I go to see him on foot; but if I am gouty and every step pains me, then those visits, on which heretofore my friend set no store, begin to have a new value; they become tokens of a very real and lively friendship: the more difficulty I have in paying them the more he will appreciate them, since one step is worth more than a mile once was! I do not say this to flatter you and fill you with self-confidence; God forbid! but only to prevent your yielding to a very dangerous temptation, that of anxiety and depression. When you are full of warmth and fervour, think nothing of your good works, which do but flow spontaneously from the source. But, on the contrary, when you feel dry, dull, cold, almost helpless, then abide in patient faith under God's Hand; confess your weakness, turn to His never-failing Love, and, above all, never mistrust His Help. Be sure it is very profitable to the soul to feel stripped of all visible stay, and reduced to cry out, "In Thy Sight shall no man living be justified."

Persevere in your onward path, in God's Name, though you may feel as if you had not strength or courage to put one foot before the other. If human courage fails you, all the better; resignation to God will not fail you in your helplessness. S. Paul said, "When I am weak then am I strong." And when he besought deliverance from his infirmity, God answered, "My strength is made perfect in weakness." Let yourself be perfected by the experience of your imperfection, and by humble recourse to Him Who is the strength of the weak. Try quietly in your meditation to seek whatever will promote recollection; do not harass yourself. Soothe your imagination, which is one while excitable, the next exhausted; make use of whatever will tend to calm you and to promote a familiar loving communion with God. Whatever is most comforting to you in this way will be most profitable. "Where the Spirit of God is, there is liberty."[1] Such liberty is to be found in simply following such leadings as draw you closest to the Beloved One. Your inner poverty will often recall the consciousness of your misery: God in His Goodness will not suffer you to lose sight of your own unworthiness, and that will speedily bring you back to His Feet. Be of good cheer,—God's Work can only be done through self-renunciation. I pray that He would uphold, comfort, impoverish you, and teach you the full meaning of His Own words, "Blessed are the poor in spirit."

[1] 2 Cor. iii. 17.

XCI

HOW TO USE SEASONS OF SPIRITUAL PEACE.

I AM very glad that your retreat has been so satisfactory, and that God gives you so much inward as well as outward peace. I pray that He Who has begun this good work in you may fulfil it to the day of the coming of Christ. It only needs now that you should make use of these peaceful days to grow in recollection. You ought to sing with your whole heart the *Amen* and *Alleluia* which re-echo in the Heavenly Jerusalem,—this is a token of continual acquiescence in God's Will, and unreserved sacrifice of yours to His. At the same time you should hearken inwardly to God, with a heart free from all the flattering prejudices of self-love, so that you may faithfully receive His Light as to the veriest trifles which need correction. Directly that He points these out, we must yield without argument or excuse, and give up whatever touches the jealous love of the Bridegroom without reserve. Those who yield in this manner to the Spirit of Grace will see imperfection in their purest deeds, and an inexhaustible fund of refined evil in their hearts. All this leads them in self-abhorrence to cry out that God Alone is good. They strive to correct themselves calmly and simply, but continuously, stedfastly, and that all the more because their heart is undivided and peaceful. They reckon on nothing as of themselves, and hope only in God; they give way neither to self-delusion nor laxity. They know that God never fails us, though we so often fail Him. They yield themselves wholly to grace, and above all things dread any resistance thereof. They blame themselves without being discouraged, they bear with themselves while striving to amend.

XCII.

ON THE PROSPECT OF DEATH IN OLD AGE.

I FULLY understand that age and infirmity make you look at death from a much more serious point of view than when you only contemplated it as an afar off thing. The vague, distant prospect which comes from time to time during a busy life, amid many distractions, is but as a dream; but death becomes a very different and far more real matter when you contemplate it in solitude and old age. It costs one little to accept it from afar and generally, but to give one's self up deliberately, with a calm gaze on approaching death, is a much greater struggle.

One must face one's end, notwithstanding the repugnance nature has to so doing. M. Olier during his last days used to take up his own hand and say, "Body of sin, thou wilt soon go to corruption. O Eternity, thou art indeed very near me!" It is not a question of rejoicing at the prospect of death; such joy does not depend on ourselves; many great Saints have not experienced it. Let us be satisfied with what does depend upon our own free will upheld and strengthened by grace. And this is, not to hearken to the promptings of nature, but to accept heartily that in which we are unable to rejoice. Nature must shrink from the bitter cup, but let the inner being say with our Dear Lord: "Nevertheless not what I will, but what Thou wilt." S. Francis de Sales distinguishes between consent and feeling (*consentir et sentir*). We are not masters of our own *feeling*, but we are by God's Grace masters of our *consent*.

Wait patiently till death comes, without letting yourself dwell sadly upon it. We are waiting for death when we try to be detached from everything; when we humble ourselves quietly over all our smallest faults with an earnest longing to correct them; when we live in God's Presence; when we are simple, docile, patient in sickness; when we give ourselves up to the Spirit of Grace to be guided solely thereby; in short, when we strive to die wholly to self, before actual death itself comes. Use your faults to your own humiliation, bear with your neighbour, ignore the forgetfulness of man,—the One True Friend, the Spouse of your heart, will never forget you.

XCIII.

ON SOME DIFFICULTIES OF TEMPERAMENT.

You are good; you want to be better, and you are making great efforts in the details of life; but I am afraid that you are encroaching rather too much upon the inner life in order to adapt it to the demands of society, and that you are not sufficiently denying the very inmost self. When we fail thoroughly to attack the internal stronghold of self-will concerning those things we love best, and most jealously, I will tell you what ensues: on the one side, great impetuosity, sharpness, and hardness of that same self-will; on the other hand, a scrupulous notion of symmetrical rule, which resolves itself into a mere observance of *les bienséances*. Thus externally comes great restraint, and internally a very lively state of rebellion—an altogether intolerable struggle.

· Try, then, to work a little less from outside, and a little more from within. Take the most keen affections which hold sway in your heart, and place them without condition or reserve in God's Hands, to be crushed and slain by Him. Resign to Him your natural haughtiness, your worldly wisdom, your pride in the greatness of your house, your dread of disrespect or want of consideration in the world, your sharp severity towards whatever is unseemly. I am less afraid of your temper than of other things: you know and mistrust it; in spite of good resolutions it carries you away, and in consequence it involves humiliation; and thus it will tend to counteract other and more dangerous faults. I should be less grieved to see you pettish, cross, brusque, wanting in self-command, and as a result thoroughly ashamed of yourself, than strictly correct and irreprehensible in all externals, but fastidious, haughty, harsh, hard, ready to take offence, self-sufficient.

Seek your real strength in prayer. This kind of human strength and rigid observance of detail in which you delight will never cure you. But accustom yourself in God's Sight, and through experience of your incurable weakness, to compassion and forbearance towards the imperfections of others. Real prayer will soften your heart and make it gentle, pliable, accessible, kindly. Would you like God to be as critical and hard towards you as you often are towards your neighbour? You are very strict in externals, and very lax inwardly; and while so jealously watchful over exterior graces, you have no scruple in letting things inward languish, or in secret resistance to God. You fear God more than you love Him. You want to pay Him with acts, for which you expect a receipt, instead of giving Him your all unreservedly. They who give all unreservedly need no accounts. You indulge in certain half-concealed clingings to your grandeur, your reputation, your comforts. If you really look into the state of things between God and your soul, you will find that there are certain limits beyond which you refuse to go in offering yourself to Him. People often hover around such reservations, making believe not to see them, for fear of self-reproach, —guarding them as the apple of the eye. If one were to break down one of these reservations, you would be touched to the quick, and inexhaustible in your reasons for self-justification,—a very sure proof of the life of the evil. The more you shrink from giving up any such reserved point, the more certain it is that it needs to be given up. If you were not fast bound by it, you would not make so many efforts to convince yourself that you are free.

It is but too true that these and the like frailties hinder God's work in us. We move continually in a vicious circle round self, only thinking of God in connection with ourselves, and making no progress in self-renunciation, lowering of pride, or attaining simplicity. Why is it that the vessel does not make way? Is the wind wanting? Nowise; the Spirit of Grace breathes on it, but the vessel is bound by invisible anchors in the depths of the sea.

The fault is not God's; it is wholly ours. If we will search thoroughly, we shall soon see the hidden bonds which detain us. That point in which we least mistrust ourselves is precisely that which needs most mistrust.

Do not bargain with God with a view to what will cost you least and bring you in most comfort. Seek only self-denial and the Cross. Love, and live by love alone. Let Love do whatsoever He will to root out self-love. Do not be content to pray morning and evening, but live in prayer all day long; and just as through the day you digest your meals, so all day long, amid your varying occupations, digest the sustenance of love and truth which you have imbibed in prayer. Let that continual prayer, that life of love, which means death to self, spread out from your fixed seasons of prayer as from a centre over whatever you do. All should become prayer, that is, a loving consciousness of God's Presence, whether it be social intercourse or business. Such a course as this will insure you real, lasting peace.

XCIV.

TO A LADY RECOVERING FROM SICKNESS.

. . . God grant that country air, gentle exercise, and thorough mental rest may restore you perfectly. As to myself, I am merely a walking, talking skeleton, which can eat and sleep but little; my occupations overwhelm me, and I never go to bed without leaving a large arrear of work undone. A vast diocese is a crushing burden when one is sixty-three! I have too much to do, and you perhaps have not quite enough; but your wisdom is to know how to occupy yourself. Delude yourself, Madame,—invent occupations to rouse yourself. Days are long, even when years are short, and you must shorten your days by dealing with yourself as with a child; such childishness is real wisdom. Remember that if you were now mixing in the best society, you would be doing no more real good than in the dulness and flatness of your present solitude; you would hear a great deal of evil talk; you would see a great many very contemptible, worthless people who bear distinguished names; you would be surrounded by snares and bad examples; you would feel the shafts of malignant envy, as well as your own frailty; you would have many faults with which to reproach yourself. It is true that you would seem to be in greater abundance, but it would really be only a perilous superfluity, with which vanity would deal; and you would not think seriously either of God, or of yourself, or of death or eternity; you would be as others are, enslaved, intoxicated, hardened. Is it not better to abide, albeit in dulness, a while away from the world and under God's Hand, learning to appreciate the hopes of religion, and detachment from the false prosperity from which you are torn? Of a truth, Madame, the counsel I give you is what I very heartily apply to myself. The world's pleasures are but vanity. It is full of thorns, of troubles, of cowardly, deceitful, detestable doings, and one must be very much spoilt by it all if we find it so hard to be kept at a distance from it. As to expenditure, I should feel rich if I had only the two thousand francs yearly which I had in my early days. Throw off the bondage of superfluity, be rich without money, and be thankful to esteem lightly whatever is lacking for the Love of God.

XCV.

COMBINED EXACTITUDE AND FREEDOM.

IT seems to me desirable that you should combine great exactitude with great liberty. The first will cause you to be faithful, the latter courageous. If you aim at being exact without freedom, you will fall into scruples and bondage; if, on the other hand, you affect freedom without exactness in duty, you will soon yield to negligence and laxity. Mere exactness in the fulfilment of duty narrows heart and mind; mere liberty stretches them too widely. They who have no experience in God's ways do not believe it possible to combine the two virtues. By being exact they understand living in a state of constraint and harass, in a restless, scrupulous timidity which deprives the soul of all rest, causes it to see sin lurking everywhere, and so narrows its horizon that it never can shake off a perpetual cavilling about every trifle, and scarcely ventures to breathe. By freedom they mean having a very lax conscience, ready to pass over detail; being content to avoid serious faults, and calling serious nothing save gross crimes; indulging freely in whatever is acceptable to self-love, and taking comfort under very considerable license as to the passions in the thought that they meant no great harm. It was not this which S. Paul contemplated when he wrote to his children in grace, whom he was trying to train up to Christian perfection: " Ye have been called unto liberty; only use not liberty for an occasion to the flesh."[1]

It seems to me that real liberty consists in obeying God in all things, and in following the light which points out our duty, and the grace which guides us; taking as our rule of life the intention to please God in all things; not only always to do what is acceptable to Him, but if possible what is *most* acceptable; not trifling with petty distinctions between sins great and small, imperfections and faults,—for although it may be very true that there are such distinctions, they should have no weight with a soul which is determined to refuse nothing it possesses to

[1] Gal. v. 13.

God. It is in this sense that the Apostle says, "The law is not made for a righteous man:"[1]—a burdensome, hard, threatening law, one might almost say a tyrannical, enslaving law; but there is a higher law which rises above all this, and which leads him into the true "liberty of sons,"—the law which makes him always strive to do that which is most pleasing to his Heavenly Father, in the spirit of those beautiful words of S. Augustine: "Love, and then do what you will."

And if, beyond merely this sincere desire always to do that which is best in God's Sight, you further do it cheerfully, are not depressed when you fail, but begin again a hundred times over, hope to the end for success, bear with yourself in your involuntary frailties as God bears, wait patiently for His appointed time of complete deliverance; and meanwhile go on quietly and according to your strength in the path before you without losing time in looking back; always "reaching forth unto those things which are before,"[2] not dwelling unprofitably upon depressing falls and hindrances; sorrowing over them, indeed, with humility, but putting them aside to press onwards; not putting a harsh, judicial interpretation on all surrounding you; not looking upon God as a spy watching to surprise you, or an enemy laying snares for you, but as a Father Who loves and would fain save you;

[1] 1 Tim. i. 9.   [2] Phil. iii. 13.

full of trust in His Goodness, continually invoking His Mercy, and perfectly free from any hollow confidence in yourself or any other creature;—such you will find to be the path towards, possibly, the fulfilment of perfect liberty. I earnestly advise you to tend thither.

Exactness and liberty ought to keep abreast, and if one halts with you rather than the other, I think it is liberty, although I freely confess that your exactitude has not yet reached the point I could desire; still, on the whole, I believe that you need more thrown into the side of confidence in God and enlargement of heart. Therefore I do not hesitate to say that you ought to yield wholly to the grace with which God sometimes draws you closer to Him. Do not be afraid to lose sight of self, to fix your gaze solely and as closely upon Him as He will permit, and to plunge wholly into the ocean of His Love—too happy if you could do it so entirely as never to come forth again. Nevertheless it is well, whenever God gives you such a happy disposition, to accept it with an act of humility and of loving, childlike fear, so as to make ready for fresh gifts. This is the counsel S. Teresa gives, and I think it may safely be given to you.

XCVI.

TO ONE IN RETIREMENT.

You will never take effectual care of M. . . . so well as by continuing constant in prayer. Our own spirit, however wise it may seem, spoils everything; only that of God insensibly works out the hardest things. The troubles of life overpower us; our crosses overwhelm us; we fail in patience and gentleness, or in quiet, even firmness, and so we cannot persuade others. Only God holds the hearts of men. He sustains ours, and opens that of our neighbour. Pray then continually and heartily, if you want to lead your flock safely. "Except the Lord keep the city, the watchman waketh but in vain." We can only win the Guiding Spirit by prayer, and time which seems wasted in it is our best spent time. You will gain more for the advancement of your outward duties by leaning in complete dependence upon the Spirit of Grace than by any amount of restless, over-anxious toil. If your meat is to do the Will of your Heavenly Father,[1] you will often feed by seeking that Will at its Source.

As to meditation, you can make it at different times during the day, because you have plenty of free time, and can often keep silence. Only avoid any exhaustion of

[1] John iv. 34.

brain in meditation. I thank God that you are weary of self. Nothing is more wearisome than that false stay, even to him who leans on it! Happy they who have grown weary of it, and who seek real rest in the spirit of detachment and of self-renunciation!

If you were to return to an ordinary worldly life, after having drawn so near God in retirement, you would fall greatly, and deserve to do so by corresponding so ill to grace. I hope such a misfortune will not occur. God loves you dearly, inasmuch as He refuses you any glimpse of peace half-way between the world and Himself. He calls us all to perfection, and leads us on thereto by the drawings of His Grace. "Be ye perfect, as your Father Which is in Heaven is perfect;" and therefore it is that He taught us the prayer, "Thy Will be done in earth as in Heaven." All men are called on to seek this perfection, but the greater part draw back in terror. Do not you be of those who, having tasted the manna of the desert, hanker after the leeks of Egypt. Perseverance wins the crown.

XCVII.

FORBEARANCE TO OTHERS AND TO SELF.

I HAVE always been warmly attached to you, but now my heart is touched by knowing that you have been blamed, and that you have borne remonstrance meekly. It is true that your morbid and somewhat austere disposition makes you rather too quick to perceive the faults of others, and you are apt to be impatient if they are not speedily corrected. I have for long wished you had such a forbearing, tolerant spirit as that with which M. M. adapts herself to every one's infirmities. She knows how to wait, to be pitiful, to open her heart; and she exacts nothing save what God may grant by degrees.

There are some external faults on which it would be very unwise to found one's judgment as to the interior; it would be the mistake of inexperience. I have often told you that M. . . . with all her visible imperfections, is much more advanced than some of those who are free from the like, and ready to find fault with her for them. It often happens that eager fault-finding, even with one's self, is but an untimely zeal, while God is carrying things on altogether differently; for sometimes He leaves people with certain unconquerable imperfections, in order to deprive them of all inward self-satisfaction. It would be far less real mortification to them to be corrected of certain involuntary failings than to feel that their weaknesses got the uppermost. Everything in its own time. Self-reliance even in the matter of curing one's faults fosters a hidden conceit.

Bear with your neighbours, then, and tolerate our

infirmities. Sometimes your heart shrinks when you are shocked by certain faults, and you may fancy that it is a repugnance arising from grace, while perhaps it is only your natural impetuosity which causes it. I think you need more forbearance, but I also think that your faults, like those of others, must be corrected, not by force or severity, but by dint of simply yielding to God and letting Him do as He will to enlarge your heart and supple it. Do you acquiesce in all He does, without anxiously inquiring how He will do it.

XCVIII.

ON SEEKING HELP IN INTERIOR TROUBLE.

I AM not at all surprised at your trouble,—it is natural you should feel it; only it should make you feel your helplessness, and lead you to have humble recourse to God. When you feel that your heart is sinking under trouble, be simple and frank in saying so. Do not be ashamed to let your weakness be seen, or to ask help in your urgent need. So doing you will advance in simplicity, in humility, and trustfulness,—you will go far to root out self-love, which keeps up a perpetual disguise in order to seem cheerful when it is really in despair. Furthermore, try to amuse yourself with whatever may lighten your solitude and keep off *ennui,* without exciting or dissipating yourself with worldly pleasures. If you nurse your troubles in silence they will wax stronger and finally overpower you, and the unreal courage which selflove creates will cause you a world of harm. The poison which goes into the system is mortal; that which comes forth does no great mischief. You must not be ashamed of seeing a free discharge from the sore in your heart. I take no heed whatever of certain expressions which escape you, and which are merely the utterance of suffering in spite of your real self. Enough if such sallies teach you that you are weak, and if you learn not to cherish your weakness, but bring it to the light that it may be cured.

XCIX.

ON OPENNESS AND CANDOUR.

. . . Nothing is more useful than speaking out freely. Open your heart; we heal our woes by not hugging them; we learn simplicity and yieldingness (for people are only reserved about things in which they do not mean to yield); and finally, we humble ourselves, for nothing is more humbling than to open one's heart and lay bare all one's weakness, yet nothing draws down a greater blessing.

I do not mean that you should make a systematic rule to yourself of always telling all you may be thinking with scrupulous exactness; this would be endless, and you would for ever be uneasy for fear of having forgotten something. Enough, so long as you keep back nothing out of untruthfulness or the false shame of self-love, which would never willingly show anything but its fair side; if you never intend to keep back anything;—grant thus much, and you may safely say less or more, as occasion and inclination serve. Although I am very busy, and perhaps often very dry, such simple truthfulness will never weary me; on the contrary, it will increase my readiness and zeal. It is not a question of the feelings, but of the will. Often our feeling does not depend at all upon ourselves. God takes it away purposely that we may feel our poverty, that we may learn to accept the cross of inner dryness, and that we may undergo the purification of clinging to Him without any sensible consolation; and then He restores us the comfort of warm feelings from time to time out of pity for our weakness.

Try to take an attitude towards God, not of forced intercourse, such as you maintain with persons towards whom you stand on ceremony and address in a mere complimentary fashion, but such as you observe towards a dear friend with whom you are under no restraint, and who is under none with you. Such friends meet and talk and listen, or are silent, content to be together saying nothing; —their two hearts rest in one another—each seems reflected in the other,—they are but as one, they do not weigh what they shall say, they insinuate nothing, bring about nothing—all comes forth in truth and love, regardless of arrangement; nothing is held back or perverted or dressed up; they are just as well satisfied one day when little has been said as another when there was plenty to say. Yet we can never be thus real with our best earthly friends as fully as we could wish, but we can be so to any extent with God, if only we will not hedge ourselves in with our own self-love. It will not do to pay Him visits, as we discharge a debt due to society; we must abide with Him in the privacy of servants, or better still, of children. Be with Him as your daughter is with you, and then you will never weary.

C.

SELF-LOVE.

WHAT I said to you hurt you so much only because I touched the most lively and sensitive point in your heart. It was the wound of your self-love which I caused to bleed. You have not dealt truthfully in what God required of you. If you had simply acquiesced in everything without listening to the pleadings of self; and if you had gone to communion in order to find that strength in our Dear Lord which you have not in yourself, you would have found real peace and benefit from your acquiescence. But that which has not been done yet may still be done, and I intreat you to lose no time in doing it.

CI.

TO A LADY, CONCERNING CERTAIN FAMILY DIFFICULTIES.

IT is true that you are too much self-absorbed, too keenly perceptive through a touchy fastidiousness, too ready to be wounded; but you must bear this inward cross as you would bear external crosses. It is much harder than they are. We suffer far more willingly from the unreasonableness of others than from our own. Pride becomes desperate; it is wounded at being wounded, and the double sting is a double evil. There is but one remedy, namely, to turn our imperfections to account in using them to our own shame and humiliation, to undeceiving ourselves, and to mistrust of self.

You ought to thank God for making you feel that the necessary work of winning M—— is one of your first duties. Renounce all your own repugnances, so as to enable yourself to teach him how to renounce his sin.

You are not mistaken in looking upon me as a sincere and unfailing friend; but you will raise a hindrance to that grace which should be your one effectual help if you do not give good heed only to seek God in me, only to see His Light as we see the sun's rays reflected through a dusky fragile glass. You will not find peace either in society or in solitude if you seek for indulgence and consolation to your irritated self-love. At such times, the sulky solitude of pride is even worse than society. If you are truthful and lowly, society will neither constrain nor irritate you, and you will seek solitude for God's Sake only.

CII.

TO A LADY WHO WAS ANXIOUS ABOUT HER SON.

As to N——, it is only weakness and dissipation. He was dissipated by the war, and other temptations found him weak and a ready prey; but I hope that experience of his own weakness will be useful to him. Let your patience with him know no bounds. Speak to him when God gives you something to say, but don't speak your own words to him. Never press him with impetuosity and worldly wisdom; never forbear out of mere diplomacy or policy. When you speak as from God your words will be full of authority, and will find a hearing.

One may speak forcibly, and yet wait patiently at the same time: his very weakness will strengthen your authority. It ought to make him feel how much he needs to mistrust himself, and so to be docile. Be firm in essential matters, on which all else depends.

I love him dearly still, and I hope that God will have only shown him the edge of the precipice, in order to cure him of his dissipation, of his love of the world, and his self-confidence. He would fall very greatly if he refused to be truthful and humble amid so much experience of his frailty and weakness. When we refuse to humble ourselves amid the humiliations which God sends on purpose to bring us to a state of lowliness and docility, we force Him to deal us heavier blows, and inflict more humbling trials. But lowliness and meekness in trial draw God's Heart to us. We can say trustfully to Him, "A broken and contrite heart Thou wilt not despise." He is moved, and cannot resist such pleadings from His children. Speak, then, according as He gives you "a mouth and wisdom." Hold the child by tender leading-strings: do not let it drop. Take care of your health, about which what I hear causes me some anxiety; take as much rest and relief as you can. The more you accept your continual crosses as daily bread, calmly and simply, the less they will damage your frail, delicate health; but forebodings and frettings would soon kill you. Do you wish to govern as God does, Who reaches from one end of the world to the other by gentleness and strength? If so, let no human considerations intermingle, and especially no self-interested plans for your family reputation.

CIII.

GOD TO BE SERVED IN ORDINARY WAYS.

WE must think how to repair the interior derangement of which you complain. The too earthly conduct of others excites all that is too earthly in ourselves, and draws us from our Abiding Centre in the life of grace; the only thing to be done is to return there with simplicity and mistrust of self. We often discover harshness, injustice, falseness, in our feelings, when brought into contact with persons who pique our self-love; but it is enough that the will does not consent to these tendencies. We ought to turn our failings to account by learning absolutely to mistrust our own heart.

I am very glad that you find yourself incapable of continuing the manner of life you have attempted. I should be greatly afraid for you if you felt so stedfast in well-doing that you were confident of perseverance; but I hope everything when I see that you honestly despair of yourself. Oh, how weak we are when we think ourselves strong! how strong in God when we feel our own weakness!

Feeling does not depend upon yourself, and love does not depend upon feeling. Your will depends upon yourself, and that is what God requires of you. Of course action must follow upon the will, but God does not often require great things of us. If you regulate your household, keep your affairs in good order, bring up your children, bear your crosses, dispense with the empty pleasures of the world, indulge your pride in nothing, repress your natural haughtiness, strive to become true, *naïve*, lowly—to be silent, recollected, given to the life which is hid with Christ in God,—these are the works which please God.

You say that you would fain bear crosses in expiation of your sins, and in token of your love of God. Be content with your actual crosses, and before seeking others try to bear them well; give no heed to your likes and dislikings, keep up a general tone of unreserved dependence upon God's Will. This is continual "death unto self." Refuse nothing to God, and do not go beforehand as to things in which you do not yet see His Will clearly. Every day will bring its own trials and sacrifices: when God wills you to pass into another state of things He will prepare you unconsciously to yourself.

CIV.

HOW TO ACCEPT ALL GOD'S DEALINGS THANKFULLY.

GOD loves you, since He is so jealous over you and so watchful in bringing home to you even your smallest faults. When you perceive any fault which indisposes you for prayer, be content to humble yourself under God's Hand, and accept this interruption of sensible grace as a deserved penance, and then be at rest. Do not seek the pleasure which you get in the society of worthy people who esteem you out of mere self-indulgence, but on the other hand do not give way to scruples about accepting such consolation when Providence sends it. Throw off the excessive keenness with which you hail all such consolations. It will suffice if your will does not yield, and if you are sincerely purposed to do without them all when they are withheld. You want to know what God requires of you in this matter? I reply, God would have you take what comes, and not run after what does not come. Accept what is given you with simplicity, looking only to God, Who thus upholds you in your weakness, and bear in faith the privation of whatever He takes away to teach you detachment. When you have learnt thus tranquilly to accept all the variableness of others towards you, as permitted by God on purpose to mould you, you will find that what pleases you will be no disturbance to your prayers, and that privations will not lead to vexation or depression.

Do not give up your fixed times for meditation, morning and evening. They are brief: you will spend them easily, half in weariness and involuntary distractions, half in return to thoughts of God. During the rest of the day let yourself go with the spirit of recollection as you are able, only observing two restrictions—one not to let it interfere with your devotional duties, and the other to take care not to tire your head and injure your very fragile health.

Go on trustfully and without fear. Fear narrows the heart, trust expands it: fear is the portion of slaves, trust of children. As to your petty weaknesses, you must accustom yourself to look at them with hearty condemnation, but without impatience or depression. And with a view to their correction, bring back your heart as often as may be through the day to the calming influences of prayer, and the familiar Presence of God.

CV.

SELF-CONSCIOUSNESS.

I QUITE understand that all your troubles come from excessive self-consciousness, and from letting yourself be too much guided by feeling. Directly that you do not find prayer a downright solace to you, you are depressed. Would you be at rest? then try to be less occupied with yourself, and more with God. Do not dissect and judge yourself, but leave yourself to be judged by the spiritual guide you have chosen. Of course we are sometimes engrossed with ourselves without meaning it, and imagination causes many relapses into this unprofitable occupation; but I do not ask what is impossible,—I shall be content if you are not voluntarily absorbed in self and do not deliberately aim at judging yourself by your own lights. Directly that you find yourself beginning to do this, turn away as from a temptation, and do not let that become intentional which was at first unconscious.

Nevertheless, do not suppose that this course which I advise is intended anywise to interfere with that vigilance over yourself which Jesus Christ teaches in the Gospel. The best possible vigilance is to watch as in God's Sight against the delusions of self-love. Now, one of the most dangerous of all these delusions is when we grow sentimental over ourselves, are perpetually self-engrossed, and feed upon ourselves with a restless, anxious care which withers and disables the heart, keeps us from realising God's Presence, and ends by hopelessly depressing and discouraging us. Say with S. Paul, "Yea, I judge not mine own self:"[1] you will watch all the better for the real correction of your faults, and the fulfilment of your duties, because of the absence of all this restless self-willed fidgetiness. Then it will be out of love of God that you will simply and quietly repress whatever you see by that clear penetrating light to be faulty and unworthy of the Beloved; you will work at conquering your failings without impatience or pettishness; you will tolerate yourself without flattery; you will accept reproof and be ready to obey. Such a line of conduct tends far more to self-renunciation than yielding to all the impatience and vexation and fancies of your own wilfulness. Moreover, when we attempt to judge ourselves by our own feelings, we take an altogether wrong standard. God only requires that which it is in our power to give, and that happens to be our will. Feeling is not in our own power—we can neither win nor lose it as we please. The most hardened sinners have at times better feelings in spite of themselves, and the greatest saints have been horribly tempted by evil feelings which they abhorred, but such feelings have tended to humble, mortify, and

[1] 1 Cor. iv. 3.

purify them. S. Paul tells us that our strength is made perfect in weakness.[1] So it is not feeling but consent[2] which makes us guilty.

Why should you suppose God is afar off because you cannot perceive Him? He is always, you may be sure, near to those whose hearts are blank and sorrowful. No pains of yours will win the conscious sweetness of His Presence. What do you seek to love? your own pleasure or the Beloved One? If the first only, then it is yourself, not God, that you seek. People often deceive themselves as to the hidden life, fancying that they are aiming at God, when self-pleasing is their real aim; and when they cease to find delight or consolation in their religious exercises, they turn from Him in disappointment. Assuredly it is never right to sacrifice that highest delight for the sake of mere earthly pleasures; but if it fails you, go on in love, and serve God in spite of weariness and disappointment. Love is of the purest when not stimulated by reward, and we often make most progress just when we think all is lost! Love suffering on Calvary is far higher than love glowing with excitement on Mount Tabor.

I don't care about seeing you a very great or very wise and good woman. I want everything on a small scale. Be a good little child.

[1] 2 Cor. xii. 9.   [2] "Pas le sentir, mais le consentir."

CVI.

FEARFULNESS.

Do not be afraid; you insult God by mistrusting His Goodness; He knows better than you what you want and are able to bear; He will never try you beyond your strength. So I repeat it; fear nothing, O you of little faith! The experience of your own weakness shows you how little you can reckon on yourself or your best resolutions. Sometimes one might suppose, to see the warmth of one's feelings, that nothing could throw one back, and .then, after having exclaimed, like S. Peter, "Though I should die with Thee, yet will I not deny Thee!" one ends like him by being frightened at a servant maid, and denying our Lord! Weak indeed we are! but while such weakness is deplorable, the realisation thereof is most useful if it strips us of all self-reliance. A weakness which we know and which humbles us is worth more than the most angelic goodness complacently self-appropriated! So be weak and depressed if God permits it; but at all events be humble, frank, and docile in your depression. Some day you will laugh at all your present fears, and will thank God for all that I say so harshly to drive you out of your timid prudence.

CVII.

TO A LADY IN SICKNESS.

I HEAR, my dear daughter, that you are ill, and I grieve for it, though I will nothing but what God wills, either for you or for myself. I am certain that you submit readily, and that when unable to give Him anything, you let Him take what He will. We can only give that which is our own, and you do not wish to call anything in this world yours; but a servant lets his master take back whatever that master had intrusted to him. Do this with your bodily life. "My soul is alway in my hand;"[1] let it pass into God's Hand as seems best to Him. We never live so truly "the life that is hid with Christ in God" as when we die to the unreal life of this world.

The true life is unknown, unintelligible, to the foolish world. Even many would-be wise and half-devout people go no farther than looking at death with a kind of abstract submission, without yielding themselves to be really detached from life by God's Hand. It is only by dying to other things that we are fitted for physical death. Some people often dwell upon the thought of death without accepting the "death unto self," whereas that makes

[1] Ps. cxix. 109.

makes people indifferent to bodily death, even when they are not specially thinking of it. S. Augustine tell us how his mother, S. Monica, said to him, "Son, for mine own part I have no further delight in anything in this life. What I do here any longer, and to what end I am here, I know not."[1] This is the mental attitude in which it is not hard to die. Self-love is unreal life; the love of God is our only true life: so soon as the last expels the first all is safe. There is no life save in this blessed death. This is the "inward man, which is renewed day by day, though the outward man perish."[2] "Do this and ye shall live," the dear Lord says.[3] Let God reign alone in your heart—let Him smash that idol "I": be as entirely absorbed by God as you have been by "I." Sacrifice that "I" to Him, and then you will find peace, liberty and life, in spite of pain, weakness, and death itself.

[1] *Conf. Lib. Fathers*, Bk. IX. x. 26. S. Monica goes on to say, "Now my wishes are accomplished. One thing there was, for which I desired to linger for a while in this life, that I might see thee a Catholic Christian before I died. My God hath done this for me abundantly, that I should now see thee withal despising earthly happiness and become His servant: what do I here?"

[2] 2 Cor. iv. 16.   [3] Luke x. 28.

CVIII.

TO THE SAME.

WE turn all our troubles to good when we bear them patiently for the love of God; but, on the other hand, we turn all that is good into evil when we use it to foster self-love. There is no real good save in detachment and resignation to God's Will. This is your time of trial; now is the time for you to give yourself up into God's Hands with unreserved confidence.

What would I not give to see you perfectly cured of your malady, and still more of the love of the world? Self-love is a hundredfold more malignant than small-pox, the venom lurks so deep within! I pray for you with all my heart.

CIX.

TO ONE IN GREAT TROUBLE.

EVERYTHING combines to try you; but God, Who loves you, will not suffer you to be tried above that you are able to bear. He will use the trials for your progress. Still you must not pry curiously even into this, but remember that God's Hand is none the less powerful when it is invisible. His workings are for the most part out of sight: we should never really die to self if we always saw His Hand visibly succouring us. At that rate He would sanctify us amid life, and all spiritual gifts; not in crosses, darkness, privation, death. Our dear Lord did not say, "If any one will come after Me, let him be richly clothed, let him be satiate with delights, like S. Peter on Mount Tabor, let him rejoice in himself and in Me, and trust to his spiritual perfection." No; He said, "If any one will come after Me, this is the road by which he must pass: he must renounce himself, he must take up his cross and follow Me, along the edge of precipices which seem to bristle with death." S. Paul speaks of our craving to be "clothed upon," but before we are so clothed by Jesus Christ we must be "unclothed."[1]

So then let yourself be stripped of all to which self clings, the better to receive that robe made white in the Blood of the Lamb, which has no purity save His own. Happy the soul which has nothing of its own, and shines solely through His Light. O bride, never so beautiful as when without ornament of thine own, as when wholly His!

Remember that the great seducer of all is "I": it seduces more souls than even Eve's tempter the serpent! Blessed is that soul which listens so devoutly to God's Voice as to forget to heed and pity self!

[1] 2 Cor. v. 4.

I would that I could be with you, but God does not suffer it. Or say rather that God brings us much nearer in Himself, the Centre of all that are His, than if we were in the same place. I am near you in spirit, I share your trials and your languor. . . . But you must die to yourself in order that Christ may live in you.

CX.

TO ONE SUFFERING FROM JEALOUSY.

You are pleased out of jealousy at the faults which try you most in M——: you are more annoyed by her good qualities than by her faults. All this is very horrible and unworthy; but it is what proceeds out of your heart, and God lets you realise it to teach you how rightly to esteem yourself, and never to reckon upon your own goodness. Your self-love grows desperate when you find yourself yielding to such vehement, shameful jealousy on the one hand, and on the other, full of distractions, weariness, and coldness for the things of God. But God often carries on His work in souls by the emptying them of self, by dint of taking away every possible resource left to self-conceit and complacency. You want to feel good, upright, strong, incapable of doing wrong? If you did so feel, you would be all the worse from that very impression. You need to feel abject, to know yourself to be bad, unjust,—to see nothing but weakness in yourself, to abhor yourself, mistrust yourself, having no hope save in God, and withal patiently to bear with yourself. Moreover, as these things which trouble you are after all only involuntary feelings, enough if your will does not consent to them, for thus you will gain the humiliation without really entertaining such evil thoughts.

Do not give up communicating: communion is the best remedy for the weakness of souls in temptation who long to live in Jesus Christ in spite of all the efforts of self-love. 'Live on Jesus Christ, and live for Him. The chief matter for you is not strength, but lowliness. Let yourself be brought low,—keep back nothing out of human wisdom and earthly courage. Learn to bear with others by dint of having so much to bear with in yourself. You fancied you had full control of yourself, but experience shows you that a moody, peevish, uncertain self-love has control of you. I hope that henceforth you will give up the notion of guiding yourself, and let yourself be wholly guided by God.

CXI.

THE RESTLESSNESS OF SELF-CONCEIT.

You want to be perfect, and to feel that you are so, and under those conditions you would be at peace. But real peace in this life must be attained with a full view of one's own imperfections, neither slurred over nor tolerated, but, on the contrary, heartily condemned. Then one bears the humiliation of one's frailty in peace, because there is no more clinging to self. One is more sorry for one's own faults than for those of others, not out of a merely selfish spirit, but because it is one's business to correct, conquer, abase one's self, in order that God's Will may be perfected in one's self. The mental attitude which you need to cultivate is faithful attention to the light thrown upon your own faults, without harbouring any of the restless fretfulness which would so soon renew your old troubles. Whatever comes to you in a quiet, simple manner is God's Light guiding you; but all argument and disturbance of your own raising must be gradually put away while you turn lovingly to God.

Try not to vex yourself with forestalling the future any more than with fretting over the past. When a real doubt arises as to your duty, try to solve it, but do not seek to raise doubts. Rather resign yourself to God, and do the best you can for the present moment.

When a sacrifice is made, do not dwell upon it; and as to those which you foresee, believe that God shows them you afar off that you may learn how to accept them. When you have once done so, there is no more to do at present; if the actual call comes ultimately, then is the time for acting upon your acceptance.

CXII.

TO A LADY. ON THE DEATH OF HER HUSBAND.

It is a sad consolation to tell you that I sympathise deeply with your grief, but it is all that earthly friends have power to do: for all else you can only turn to God. And indeed, Madame, I very heartily turn to Him, the Comforter of the afflicted, the Stay of the weak. I ask Him, not to take away your grief, but to turn it to your good, to give you strength to bear up under it, not to let it overwhelm you. Great and grievous sorrow is the sovereign remedy to the most dangerous evil of our nature, for amid such sorrow the great mystery of Christianity, the inward crucifixion of the natural man, takes place. Then it is that all the power of grace is developed, and its most real work, that of rooting out self, achieved; otherwise the love of God is not in us. We must go forth from out of self before we can give ourselves to God; and in order thus to force us out of self, it needs some deep heart's wound which shall turn all that is of this world to bitterness for us. Then the heart, wounded in its tenderest point, torn from its sweetest, purest, loveliest moorings, realises that it can find no rest within, and bursts forth to cast itself upon God.

And this truly is the sovereign cure for the grievous ills with which sin overwhelms us. The cure seems a severe process, but then the disease is very deep-seated. It is the true support of Christians in their sorrows. God parts two people bound together by the most sacred bonds, and in truth He sends a blessing to both, for the one He takes to His own Eternal Glory, and by this healing sorrow He saves her who is left a little while in this world. This is what God has done for you. May His Holy Spirit kindle your faith, and fill your soul with His Truth. I ask it earnestly for you, Madame; and as I have great belief in the prayers of God's afflicted children, I intreat you to pray for me amid your sorrow. Your charity will tell you what I need, and lead you to ask it fervently.

CXIII.

TO THE DUCHESSE DE CHEVREUSE,[1] SOME TIME AFTER HER HUSBAND'S DEATH.

. . . Your letter cost me some tears. Sorrow for your loss is an addition to my own sorrow, but amid all our

---

[1] The Duc de Chevreuse was "not loved, but adored," by his family, Saint Simon says, and especially by his wife, who was her-

grief we must not lose sight of God's designs. He has sought at once to reward him whom we mourn and to teach us greater detachment; He has taken from us an earthly stay on whom we leant too much even in striving to glorify Him. He vouchsafes sometimes to be jealous of His own best tools, and will have us seek the fulfilment of His Work through Himself only.

The chief lesson God means to teach you in this trial is a practical one,—that you were not yet as detached from earthly things as you flattered yourself you were. We never know ourselves till the time of trial comes, and God only sends such trial to undeceive us as to our

self a person of most remarkable piety and spiritual attainments. Saint Simon describes her unworldliness and attractive goodness. After her husband's death she could not be induced to return in any degree to the world, beyond granting the interviews sought by Louis XIV., who had always held her in great admiration. After the King died "she set herself free from all worldly claims, and lived entirely amid a very narrow circle of friends and relations. She slept little, spent a long morning in devotion and good works, gathered her family around her at meals, which were always refined without being sumptuous, and always received as though not expecting the attentions which the world never ceased to pay her, though she made no return. She was like a patriarch in her family —their delight, their centre, their common bond. No woman was ever so justly adored by all her belongings, or so respected by the world to the end of her life, which reached to over eighty, in full health of mind and body,—a life even then too short for her family and friends. She died in 1752, an object of public veneration, as bravely and devoutly as she had seen her husband die."—SAINT SIMON, vol. xix. p. 161.

superficial detachment. God suffered S. Peter's terrible fall in order to undeceive him as to the real nature of a certain outward fervour and very frail courage on which he was most vainly relying. If you had only your outward cross to bear, however heavy or sharp it might be, it would not undeceive you as to the reality of your detachment; on the contrary, the more overwhelming the outward cross, the greater your inward satisfaction at not yielding under it, and so self-confidence is fostered, and a very dangerous delusion. The Cross only teaches us our real weakness and frailty when within we feel all dark and cold, while from without we are sorely pressed. The thing is to face and realise our inward weakness, then our utter poverty becomes a real treasure, and "having nothing we possess all things."

Let us heartily unite ourselves to him we mourn. He sees us, he feels for our needs, he prays for us. He still speaks to you in the words he so often used while yet among us, "Live by faith only; think nothing of your regular life or your many good deeds; bear patiently with the consciousness of your imperfections; give yourself up to God; never give ear to your own imaginations; hearken solely to the Spirit of Grace." This is what he used to say; this is what he still says to you. So far from having lost him, you will find him nearer, more closely bound to you, more available to comfort you, more helpful in leading you with his counsels, if you can learn to realise his companionship through faith instead of the visible, daily companionship which was so sweet to you.

Take care of your health for the sake of your family, which greatly needs you. May the courage of true faith sustain you. It is a courage which makes no boast, and which does not inspire a conscious strength whereon to rely. They who have it have no self-reliance, and yet they never lack anything in time of need: their poverty is true riches. If they unconsciously go astray, they turn it to account in humiliation, they continually return to their true centre point by consenting to whatever is a laying aside of self. They throw themselves upon God by absolutely refusing to trust themselves. And so by degrees recollection, silence, a perpetual reliance on grace in every detail, an ever-growing hidden life through death unto self, become as a very second nature to them. And thus, "having nothing, and yet possessing all things," such souls find again all that they once fancied they had lost, and beyond that, the closest, truest union with God.

CXIV.

TO THE YOUNG DUCHESSE DE MONTEMART.[1]
ON SOME DOMESTIC TROUBLES.

CAMBRAI, *Aug.* 4, 1706.

IT seems to me that the chief thing for you is never to despair of God's Goodness, and only to mistrust yourself. The more we mistrust ourselves, and look to God only for the correction of our faults, the more it will be achieved, but it will not do to reckon upon God without working hard one's self. Grace only works effectually in us when we, on our side, work heartily too. You must watch, be strict with yourself, shun self-deceit, receive the most humiliating rebukes patiently, and only count yourself to be dealing faithfully with God when you are making daily practical sacrifices and self-denials.

As you think that you have said things to the Duke tending to set him against his mother, you must endeavour to put this right; but do it quietly and gradually. It is very important that her son should not be in anywise estranged from such a good mother, who loves him dearly, and is so devoted to his real interests. She may

---

[1] Henriette de Beauvilliers, who married her cousin, and was living with her mother-in-law (likewise aunt), Mme. de Montemart. This lady, as well as her sisters, had been objects of Fénelon's affection and interest from their childhood. The *Education des Filles* was written at their parents' request.

from time to time do too much or too little, as easily happens to the wisest and best-intentioned people; but take it all in all, you seldom find any one truly religious and right-minded in all respects. She may sometimes be a little quick with you concerning what she considers your real good; but she loves you,—that I can say from my own knowledge,—and what you feel to be excessive is but an excess of affection. Indeed, you ought to strive diligently to draw the mother and son together, both for his sake and your own; but try to do it without vexing and exciting yourself. If you have committed some serious faults in this matter, as would appear to be the case from your letter to me, you must bear your inward humiliation without being disheartened. Try henceforward to avoid anything which could tend to the repetition of such errors, and be careful to neglect no opportunity of repairing the past. I have noticed one excellent point in you, and that is your openness with your mother-in-law. Keep this up,—tell her everything, whatever it may cost you: you know by experience how she will receive it, and God's Blessing will be on such straightforward simplicity. You see how good He is to you, little as you have corresponded to His correction. Would you misuse His Patience, and turn it against Himself, by treating His Mercies with contempt? Nor will it suffice to tell everything; you must do so at once, be perfectly sincere from the first, and not wait for God to wrest from you that which you cannot withhold. How glad I shall be if I can hear that God has opened your heart, and taught you to mistrust your imagination; and that you have learned to cast aside your indolence, and go to work steadily at all your duties. Then you would find as much freedom and peace as now you have anxiety, depression, and uncertainty.

You see by the freedom with which I speak how sincerely I am devoted to you.

CXV.

TO THE DUCHESSE (DOUAIRIÈRE) DE MONTEMART.
ON BEARING REPROOF.

CAMBRAI, Aug. 22, 1708.

. . . . I EARNESTLY desire that you may be at peace within. You know that peace can only be found in lowliness, and that lowliness is only real so long as we suffer ourselves to be abased under God's Hand, time after time, as He wills. The means which He most frequently uses are contradiction and blame from others, and our own inward weakness. We must learn to bear both the one and the other, from without and from within. We become really lowly when we are no longer surprised either at receiving censure from others, or at feeling incorrigible within. Then everything overrules us like little children, and we are willing to be overruled; we are conscious that others are right, but feel helpless in ourselves to amend. By this time we expect nothing of ourselves, and have no hope save in God; and then the reproofs of others, however hard or harsh they be, seem less than we deserve; and if we find them hard to bear, we are more inclined to blame our sensitiveness than to justify ourselves. So that even reproof can scarcely humble us, we are already so lowly. When we feel an inward rebellion against reproof, it shows how urgently we needed it, for indeed no reproof can benefit one unless it cuts to the quick; so the more we feel it, the more necessary we may conclude it to be.

Forgive me all my freedom, dear Duchess. God knows how much I love you, and how I feel for all your troubles. I beg your pardon if anything I have said seems harsh; do not doubt my affection, and do not think of *me* in the matter; look only to God's Hand, which has used mine as the awkward instrument wherewith to deal you a painful blow. Your pain proves that I have touched the ailing spot. Yield to God, submit unreservedly; this alone will give you rest and restore your tone. It is only what you know so well how to say to others. This is a weighty season, a very crisis. What grace will be poured out upon you, if you bear like a little child all that God is doing to humble you and strip you both of self-reliance and self-will! I intreat you to make yourself so small that you may nowhere be found!

CXVI.

TO THE SAME. IN REPLY TO SOME QUESTIONS CONCERNING SELF-KNOWLEDGE.

Oct. 11, 1710.

FEW letters ever gave me more real pleasure than your last, my dear Duchess. I thank God for leading you to write it. I am alike convinced as to your sincere intention to say everything and your incapacity to do so. So long as one has not attained perfection, one can know one's self but imperfectly. The same self-love which causes our faults is very subtle in hiding them both from ourselves and from others. Self-love cannot endure to see itself; it would die of shame and vexation! If by chance it gets a glimpse, it at once places itself in some artificial light, so as to soften the full hideousness and find some comfort. And so there will always be some remains of self-delusion clinging to us while we still cling to self and its imperfections. Before we can see ourselves truly, self-love must be rooted up, and the love of God alone move us; and then the same light which showed us our faults would cure them. Till then we only know ourselves by halves, because we are only half God's, and hold a great deal more to ourselves than we imagine or choose to see. When the truth has taken full possession of us, we shall see clearly, and then we shall behold ourselves without partiality or flattery, as we see our neighbours. Meanwhile God spares our weakness, by only showing us our own deformity by degrees, and as He gives strength to bear the sight. He only shows us to ourselves, so to say, by bits; here one and there another, as He undertakes our correction.

Spiritual guides ought not to display all people's faults to them until such time as God prepares the way. They ought to watch a failing patiently, and say nothing until He begins to speak in inward rebuke. Sometimes even it is necessary to imitate God's dealings with souls, Who often so softens His rebuke that the person rebuked feels rather as though he were accusing himself than being accused. Anything like impatient reproof from being shocked at great faults becomes a very human correction, not that of grace. Our own imperfection makes us hasty to rebuke the imperfect; and it is a very subtle and all-permeating self-love which cannot forgive the self-love of others. The stronger it is, the more critical the censor will be: there is nothing so irritating to a proud, self-willed mind, as the self-will of a neighbour; and another man's passions seem intolerably ridiculous and unbearable to one who is given up to his own. But he who is full of the love of God, on the contrary, is full of forbearance, consideration, and indulgence. He waits and adapts himself, and goes softly, one step at a time: the less self-love he has, the more he tolerates that of others, in order to heal it. No surgeon probes a wound without applying soothing ointment to the wound, or purges a sick man without nourishing him, or risks any operation save when nature indicates that the time is seasonable. And so a wise spiritual guide will sometimes wait years to give a wholesome counsel; he waits till Providence gives a favourable opportunity, and till grace makes a like preparation of the heart. If you persist in gathering fruit before it is ripe, you simply waste it all. . . .

Among our friends who are themselves imperfect there can be little perfect knowledge of us. They often judge only from certain external failings which are obvious in society, and which wound the self-love of others. Self-love is a sharp, severe, suspicious, implacable censor; and while it softens away our critics' own faults, it exaggerates ours in their eyes. As they see things from a totally different point of view from ours, they see things in us which we do not see, and they are blind to much that we do see. They see keenly enough a great deal which offends the jealous sensitiveness of their own self-love, and which ours disguises; but they do not see that within which clouds our virtues, and which offends God only.

And so their wisest judgments are but very superficial. . . .

As to recollection, I do not ask you to cultivate it *actively*, and by passive recollection I mean avoiding dissipating causes, and not encouraging your natural eagerness. Enough if you let God work in you, and do not hinder recollection by superfluous occupations which merely concern vanity or inclination. Often it is enough simply to turn aside from the natural eagerness which prompts you, and you will find yourself unconsciously returning to the influence of grace. Occupy yourself little with your neighbours' affairs; ask little, expect little of them, and do not be ready to fancy that people are wanting towards you whenever self is tempted to feel somehow affronted. Let it all pass away, and bear such annoyances as do not pass away with meekness. . . . So doing, you will accomplish whatever you have to do quietly, and without anxiety or *empressement*. . . . You will be content when you seek nothing. But to maintain such peace you must continually cast aside whatever tends to disturb it. You must often silence yourself, in order to hearken to the Master speaking within, and teaching you all His truths. He often speaks to those who listen faithfully; and when we do not hear His secret, familiar Voice within, it is a proof that we do not hush ourselves duly to hearken. His Voice is no foreign accent: God is in the soul, as the soul in the body,—a something which we cannot distinguish from ourselves, yet which we are conscious is leading, restraining, controlling us. The silence by which we hear His Voice is a trustful dependence, a recalling whenever we are conscious of wandering from Him. . . .

I see by your letter, dear Duchess, that you are convinced that our friends . . . have been greatly wanting in what is due to you. It may be so . . . but I do not believe it was intentional. . . . I am not going to make excuses for them, but I think you ought to beware of the exceeding keenness with which you have felt their conduct. A sudden change in friends is painful, and it is hard to bear;—one easily perceives a lack of courtesy or friendship. It is natural for wounded self-love to exaggerate whatever wounds it, and I think you should mistrust the opinions you may form at such a time. Indeed, I think you may go further, and believe that the malady needed a stern remedy. This total upset, your complete overwhelming, which you mention so frankly, show that your heart was very sick. The probing has been sharp; but it was needed. You may see this by the pain it has caused to your self-love. . . . You are fortunate in that God has made use of other men's faults to correct yours. What was wrong on their part has been a great mercy to you. Accept the bitterness and pain if you wish to be healed.

CXVII.

TO THE SAME. ON CROSSES.

CAMBRAI, *July* 27, 1711.

I HAVE not written to you for long, dear Duchess, but I am afraid to write by the post, and it is some time since any other opportunity offered. You do well in leaving our friends' confidence to come and go as they will. One learns to bear what is wearisome, and sensitiveness wears off when we persevere in putting aside all brooding on self. The less we expect from our neighbour the more kindly and helpful to every one we shall become. If you seek confidence, it escapes you;—leave it alone, and it is sure to come back; but I do not mean that you should not seek it merely with this object.

The heavier your crosses are the more careful you should be not to add to them. And you do add to them either by making vain efforts against Providence from without, or by other no less vain struggles within. You must be motionless beneath the Cross, keep it as long as God gives it, without trying to move it impatiently; and moreover bear it in a lowly spirit, adding to its own weight the shame of bearing it so badly. The Cross would cease to be a cross if self-love had the flattering support of believing that it was enduring manfully.

... As to myself, I spend my life in growing angry unreasonably, in talking indiscreetly, in being impatient of the importunities which vex me. I hate and despise the world, and yet it still flatters me. I feel old age creeping over me, and grow used to it, without learning real detachment from life. I find nothing real in myself, outwardly or inwardly. When I examine myself I seem to be dreaming, and see myself as a mere vision. . . . I think I have no desire to meddle with the world; I feel a sort of barrier between myself and it, which keeps me far from seeking it; and I think I should be heartily grieved if I were called back to it.

CXVIII.

TO LA SŒUR CHARLOTTE DE SAINT-CYPRIEN, CARMELITE. DANGERS OF INTELLECTUAL ATTRACTIONS.

Nov. 30.

WHAT will you say, my dear Sister? I have not had one available moment in which to read your "Life of the Blessed Jean de la Croix," but I hope soon to read it carefully. . . . What I would desire for you, dear Sister, is that you should not trust too much to intellect in your obedience. Do not obey a man because he can argue more forcibly or speak more feelingly than others, but because he is providentially ordered for you and is your natural superior, or because apart from all else you feel that he more than others is able to help you to conquer your infirmities and attain to self-renunciation. A director is of little use in teaching detachment from self when it is self-will which seeks him. O my dear Sister, how I wish I could teach you true poverty of spirit! Remember what S. Paul says: "We are fools for Christ's Sake, but ye are wise."[1] I would fain see in you no wisdom save that of grace, which leads faithful souls in the sure way when they do not yield to temper, their passions, or self-will, or to any merely natural impulse. To such as these all that the world calls talent, taste, and good reasoning is as nought.

CXIX.

TO THE SAME. ON THE SAME SUBJECT.

I CAN only repeat what I have ventured to say frequently before: Beware of your own intellectual gifts, and those of others; judge no one according to them. God, the only wise Judge, goes on a very different line; He gives the preference to children and childlike minds. Read nothing out of mere curiosity, or in order to confirm your own opinions; rather read with a view to foster a

[1] 1 Cor. iv. 10.

hearty spirit of meekness and submission. Talk little of yourself, and never save as a matter of obedience. Be as frank as a child towards your superiors. Make no count at all of your lights or extraordinary graces. Abide in simple faith, content to be obscure and unremitting in obedience to God's Commandments and the Evangelical Counsels as set forth in your Rule. Act up to whatever God may make known to you through others, and accept meekly whatever may seem strange to you. Self-forgetfulness should take the shape of crushing out self-will, not of neglecting that watchfulness which is essential to the real love of God. The greater your love, the more jealously you will watch over yourself, so that nothing may creep in unworthy of that love. This, dear Sister, is all I have to say to you: receive it in the same spirit with which I write. I ask our Lord to give you a deeper understanding of these things than anything I can say, and Himself to be all in all to you.

CXX.

TO THE SAME. SICKNESS A TRUE PENITENTIAL EXERCISE.

. . . No one can be more sorry for your sufferings than I am, and I forgive them for hindering you in your penitential exercises. Are not sickness and pain a continual penitential exercise given us by God, and infinitely better adapted to our needs by His Hand than anything we could choose for ourselves? What is to be aimed at in any penitential works save mortification of the flesh and submission of the spirit to God? As to your reading, I cannot regret the loss, so long as it pleases God to deprive you of the power to read. All the best books in the world put together cannot teach one so much as the Cross. It is better to be crucified with Jesus Christ than to read His "Sufferings;"—this last is often only an interesting study, or at best an exercise of the affections, whereas the other is the real solid fruit, and carrying out in practice the result of all our prayers and meditations. So go on bearing your pain in silence and tranquillity, dear Sister: no better meditation than union with Christ on His Cross. No one can suffer quietly for the love of God without praying most really and purely. And so you may safely let books alone; books are only useful in so far as they teach and fit us for this self-sacrificing prayer. You will remember the passage in which S. Augustine, speaking of the final moment of his conversion, says that after having read certain words of S. Paul, "No further would I read, nor needed I; for a light as it were of security was infused into my heart."[1] When God supplies inward nourishment, we do not need it

[1] *Conf.* Bk. VIII. c. xii. p. 153, *Lib. of Fathers.*

from without. The word from without is only given in order to supply that which is inward; and when God tries us by depriving us of that which is external, He makes up for the deficiency by supplying the need, and not leaving us to our own destitution. Be it yours, then, to wait silently and lovingly upon Him. Occupy your mind with whatever His Grace may suggest in meditation, to make up for what you cannot have by means of reading. Verily Jesus Christ, the Incarnate Word of the Father, is a Divine Book of teaching. Sometimes we seek merely to indulge our curiosity in reading, or to gratify our intellect; and then God weans us from such pleasure by sickness. He trains us by helplessness and a languid incapacity which is very trying and humbling to self-love. But what an excellent lesson! Where is the book which could teach one so much?

One thing I do very earnestly intreat of you is honestly to spare your strength, and to receive the alleviations afforded you as you would wish some one else to whose needs you ministered to receive them. Such simple, unaffected conduct will be a greater mortification to you than the austerities you regret, but which are out of the question. Moreover, God is better served by one who, overwhelmed with suffering, is content to be deprived of all consolation, than by those who are absorbed in the most conspicuous works. "To whom will I look, saith the

Lord, but to him that is poor and of a contrite spirit, and trembleth at My Word?"[1] The one class find their stay in their own lights, their own exertions, their own works, but God carries the other tenderly in His own Arms. Weep as much as you will over the faults which you say God brings to your mind; I like what you call your *stupidity* a hundredfold better than your fine intellectual feelings, which are a purely hollow stay. Be content with what God gives you, and that alike in every kind of vicissitude. Once more, take care both of body and mind, for both are exhausted.

CXXI.

TO LA MÈRE MARIE DE L'ASCENSION, CARMELITE (THE ARCHBISHOP'S NIECE).
ON THE DUTIES OF A SUPERIOR.

July 19, 1712.

I TRUST, my dear niece, that God, Who has called you to bear rule among your sisters, will take away all that is of your own spirit, and fill you with His Spirit to fulfil your work. God's work is to make men love Him, and to root out self, so that He alone may live in us. So your function is to mortify the creature and adore the Creator; and must you not mortify self, that you may

[1] Isa. lxvi. 2.

teach others mortification? must you not love, if you would kindle love in them? No teaching is effectual without example; no authority is endurable save in so far as it is softened by example. Begin with acting, and let your words come after that. Action speaks and persuades: mere words are purely vain. Do you strive to be the lowest, humblest, most obedient, most recollected, most detached, most regular member of your House. Obey the Rule, if you would be yourself obeyed; or better still, teach others to obey, not you, but the Rule, to which you are foremost in obedience. Do not indulge any failings, but bear patiently with every possible infirmity. Wait for those souls whose progress is slow: you run the risk of disheartening them by impatience. The more vigour you need, the more gentleness and kindness you must combine with it. Why, when the Lord's yoke is easy and light, should that of a Superior be hard or heavy? Either be a real mother in compassionate tenderness, or do not presume to fill the place of one. You must learn to put yourself by self-abnegation under the feet of all those who have placed you over their heads by election. Endure all things: it is only by means of the Cross that we can hope to acquire the grace and mind of Jesus Christ so as to win souls. Superiors who do not bear the Cross will always be barren as to the offspring of grace. A well-borne cross gives untold influence, and brings a blessing on whatever you do. S. Paul was only shown the good works he was to do, together with the sufferings he was to endure. It is only through suffering that we learn to pity and comfort others.

Consult persons of experience; say little, listen much; study much more how to get a knowledge of the hearts of those under your care and adapt yourself to their needs than to talk fluently to them. Let them see that your heart is open to them, and let every one learn by experience that they can open theirs to you with safety and comfort. Avoid every sort of harshness, and find fault, when it must be done, with kindliness and consideration. Never say more than is necessary, but say that with the fullest honesty. Let no one have cause to fear lest they should be mistaken in believing what you say. Decide slowly but firmly. Keep your eye on each person committed to your care, and follow her if she strays from you. You must learn to be all things to all God's children, so that you may gain them all. Above all, correct yourself if you would be able to correct others. Invite others to tell you your faults, and believe that what they will tell you is precisely that to which your self-esteem blinds you.

I am, my dear niece, your truly devoted, and anxious for all your best interests in our Lord, etc.

CXXII.

TO ONE ABOUT TO ENTER THE RELIGIOUS LIFE. ON INDECISION AND WEAKNESS.

I REJOICE to think of you as on the eve of a great sacrifice, wherein I trust you will find peace. But that needs to be less sought in outward condition than in the heart's disposition. So often as you attempt to look forward and make conditions with God, so often, you may be sure, He will overthrow all your plans, and you will lose all that you sought to grasp. Far better to let go everything unreservedly. God's Peace can only be found where all self-seeking and self-will are utterly thrown aside. When you cease to be eager for anything save God's Glory and the fulfilment of His Good Pleasure, your peace will be as deep as the ocean, and flow with the strength of a flood. Nothing save holding back, and the hesitation of an undecided mind, can disturb or limit that peace, which is as boundless as God Himself. You are a very Lot's wife, for ever looking back out of anxiety and mistrust. What you are leaving needs neither retrospect nor regret; let it drop out of your sight as well as from your hands. The indecision of your mind, which cannot be stedfast when things are settled, causes you a great deal of utterly useless trouble, and hinders you in God's Ways. You do not go on, you simply go round and round in a circle of unprofitable fancies.

One cannot call you headstrong, for no one ever met truth with less resistance, but your docility only lasts while one is speaking to you, and then you relapse into indecision. The present time is a sort of crisis, in which you must try to make a thorough change. So give no further heed to yourself, but act steadily up to your decision. If you hearken to the promptings of self, you invite temptation. To-morrow you will be no longer your own,—for long, indeed, you have had no right to call yourself so. God takes you wholly as His, and you—half draw back. You lack courage. A false wisdom and selfishness lower your standard. The moment that you think of nothing save God's Will you will not know fear, and there will be no hindrance in your way. Cast aside all earthly impulses, and so doing you will spare yourself much inward anxiety and much outward indiscretion.

God would have you wise, not in your own conceits, but in His Wisdom; He will guide you in true wisdom, not through your own imaginations, but rather by utterly casting them aside. When you cease to act upon impulse you will be free from self-conceit. The movements of grace are simple, frank, childlike. Impetuous nature imagines and talks largely; grace scantily, because it is calm and recollected. It adapts itself to various temperaments, and is all things to all men; it is universally plastic and yielding, because it clings to nought of self, but only seeks to help others. It knows how to proportion, to restrict, to mould itself to the needs of others. It is willing to be rebuked and corrected; and, above all, it knows how to hold its tongue, and only say what its neighbour can bear, whereas nature is for ever pouring out the overflow of inconsiderate zeal.

I shall ask God to treat you as wholly His Own, and to spare you in nothing which can promote His Glory. Woe to those weak, timid, selfish souls who expect to be indulged, and to put a limit to God's Grace. He does not reign by halves: His Will must be done on earth as it is in Heaven, and whatever is not offered to God in that spirit must needs pass through the fire of purification ere it can be acceptable in His Eyes.

CXXIII.

TO A NOVICE ABOUT TO BE PROFESSED.

I LONG to know how you have prospered in your retreat, while awaiting the day which you fear so much, and which is really so little to be feared. You will find out that the phantoms which scare you from a distance are nothing at all when you draw near. When S. Teresa took her vows, she says that she fell into a state of convulsive trembling, and felt as if all her bones were out of joint. "Learn from my example," she says, "to fear nothing in giving yourself to God." In fact that first terror was followed by a peace and sanctity which are yet our marvel and admiration.

I would rather have you take eight hours sleep, and pay God with some other coin by day. He does not require you to watch more than your strength permits; but He does require a simple, docile, recollected mind, a heart yielding to His Will, generous in its unlimited acceptance thereof, ready to do and suffer all things, wholly detached from the world and from self. This is the real pure immolation of the whole man; all else is not himself, but his rude husk.

Prostrate yourself before the Child Jesus with the Magi. Giving up your will (which indeed is not yours to give), you will make a more precious offering than all the gold and perfumes of the East. Offer it, but unreservedly and without recall. They who give thus receive abundantly, while those who keep back anything lose greatly. The faithful soul has nothing left, not even himself. You must not fret over your faults so long as you do not cherish them, or any secret inclination to persist in them. All such reservations hinder grace and keep the soul from reaching forth to God. If you lay all your failings unreservedly at God's Feet, He will scorch them up as fire consumes straw; He will make them serve to humble, crucify, confound you; He will wrest all self-reliance and conceit from you by their means; and then, when He has smitten you, He will burn the rod. Be of good cheer,—love, endure, be patient and yielding in His Hand.

CXXIV.

TO A LADY. ON CONFESSION AND COMMUNION.[1]

MADAME,—In reply to your questions concerning confession and communion, I reply that the Eucharist was instituted in the form of Bread, that is to say, of our most familiar food, and the Fathers call it "daily bread." The

---

[1] Fénelon's meaning in this, as in another letter on "Frequent Communion" (*Letters to Men*, p. 319), must not be misunderstood. He is affirming and proving that the Christian's privilege and blessing is to receive the Blessed Sacrament *daily*, and that to abstain from so receiving, and only to assist at Mass, the celebration thereof, is to forfeit our privilege. But he by no means condemns the practice of assisting at such celebration *after* having received, as a separate act of thanksgiving and prayer, or where sickness and infirmity render communion at a proper hour impossible. This seems too obvious to need stating. In other letters he tells people to come to a late celebration under such circumstances to *assist*. Here he is only arguing against the notion that it is more reverent to abstain from *very frequent* communion.

primitive Christians broke this sacred bread " daily with gladness and singleness of heart."[1] S. Chrysostom says, " In vain we offer the mysteries, if none partake thereof." Assisting at mass without taking part in it by communion is but half a work; so doing we only half fulfil the intention of Jesus Christ in the institution of this Sacrament. Nothing but our own unworthiness ought to exclude us from the communion of our daily bread. All Christians are called to it, and they offend against the sacrament when they deprive themselves thereof. Our whole life ought to tend to prepare us to receive Holy Communion daily. The Eucharist is offered by the priest that the faithful may live by it. The one action bears strict reference to the other; and there is something wanting to the sacrifice when the laity draw back as though forbidden to approach the altar, not daring to eat the Victim offered for them. Yet modern ideas are very far off these purer views. People are somewhat scandalised at a priest who does not say Mass daily, and yet they are surprised to see a layman communicate every day in the week. But if the layman be leading a good Christian life, he may and ought to communicate daily if able, just as a good priest, if able, may and ought to offer the sacrifice daily. I should make no exception save of those persons who are either subject to a Com-

[1] Acts ii. 46.

munity Rule, where everything is laid down for them, or to such worldly engagements as make caution necessary. To this I must add, that such persons as cling to their failings and voluntarily indulge in venial sin are unworthy of this daily communion. But as to simple, upright souls, who are willing to do all they can to improve, who are humble and docile, the daily bread is unquestionably theirs by right. Their involuntary failings, so far from excluding them, do but increase their need to be fed with the Bread which strengtheneth.

Nothing, then, can be more opposed to the institution of the Sacrament and to the spirit of the Church than to show respect to the Eucharist by receiving it seldom. Provided men be living in a state of purity, the true reverence is to receive it frequently. I know men cannot say "I am pure;" but we must not judge ourselves, we must let ourselves be guided by a pious, discreet counsellor.

The rule for confession is just the contrary to that for communion. Communion is food essential to life; the more one takes it the more one is nourished and strengthened. But confession, on the contrary, is a medicine, and one ought to try to diminish one's need of it. I know very well that the need will never altogether cease, for we shall always commit faults so long as we live, but at least we must endeavour to lessen the necessity which we cannot altogether do away with.

The power which Jesus Christ gave to His ministers to bind and loose, to forgive and to retain sins, is absolute and without restriction. But they cannot absolve secret sins which are not made known to them. Therefore this ministry implies the avowal of sins, either public or at least private. This is confession. When it is only auricular (*i.e.* made to the ear of one), it is the least that can be required. But, one way or other, the sinner must accuse himself. As to the minister, he has unrestricted power to remit all sins, and so much the more clearly venial sin. It does not appear that in early times people confessed themselves as frequently of these venial sins as is now the custom among us. The Fathers (especially S. Augustine) say that such sins are remitted by the Lord's Prayer, the fasts of the Church, and by almsgiving. But, above all, such sins are wiped out by the Love of God, that consuming fire which shrivels up our imperfections as natural fire consumes straw. Many venial sins are remitted to that soul which loves much. When we read the lives of the early Fathers of the Church, we find their historians relating their death with circumstantial detail, without mentioning the frequent confessions we now use. This was because they lived lives of great purity, and it does not seem that in those days men made regular confession of those venial sins which no one would cherish who truly loves God.

I acknowledge that the present use of the Church is otherwise. But this change of discipline need not surprise us. The power to remit venial sin is still given to the priest, so that the faithful may resort to its help whenever so doing is profitable to him. Many saints have done thus with the happiest results; many souls find abundant purification through this means. It were a shameful wrong to deprive the number of tender consciences which need this consolation, this supply of grace, of it. Of course we must guard against letting it become a mere habit, a treacherous comfort, a mere unprofitable relief to the heart. People sometimes are tempted to think that all is done when they have told their sins; others rely on the efficacy of absolution to excess (*i.e.* regardless of amendment of life); others find a certain pleasure and self-satisfaction in talking about themselves, perhaps to a confessor of their own choice, and to whom they feel a great attraction. And then this practice of confession becomes just as easy and soothing to such persons who use it in a mere routine, which takes the place of all else to them, as it is a sharp discipline to sinners who rarely use it. Wise, discreet confessors ought to be able to judge of their penitents' needs, and be guided by the profit derived from their confessions as to their more or less frequency. I must venture to say that, generally speaking, this is a matter which is not treated with sufficient weight and seriousness. As to upright, enlightened people, it seems to me that they do well to bear in mind two things,—one to go to confession as often as seems needful, or even beyond that strict limit, as a matter of example; and the other to conform to the present discipline of the Church, and try to profit by it by coming to confession with a lowly, teachable heart.

CXXV.

ON THE EMPLOYMENT OF TIME.

I QUITE understand that what you want of me is not to convince you of the great duty of using time rightly;—grace has taught you that long since. One is happy in having to deal with souls who have so to say accomplished half their journey; but do not suppose I mean to flatter you,—you have still a long way to go, and there is a wide difference between the mind's conviction and the right disposition of the heart, taking shape in diligent, dutiful practice.

Nothing has been commoner at all times, or now, than to meet with souls who are most perfect and saintly in precept. But "ye shall know them by their fruits," the Saviour of the world has said; and this is the only sure rule, if it be fairly dealt with;—by this we must judge ourselves. Time bears a very different aspect at different seasons of one's life, but there is one maxim which applies equally to all seasons, namely, that none should go by uselessly,—that all time forms part of the order, a link of the chain of God's Providence as regards our salvation,—that every season carries with it various duties of God's own appointing, and concerning the discharge of which we must give account to Him, since from the first to the last moment of life, God never means us to look upon any time as purposeless, either to be used as our own apart from Him or lost. The important thing is to know how He would have us use it. And this is to be learnt, not by restless, fidgety eagerness, which is much more calculated to confuse than enlighten us, but by hearty submission to those God has set over us, and by a pure, upright heart, simply seeking God, and diligent in resisting the deceits and wiles of self-love as fast as it perceives them. For remember, we lose time not only by doing nothing, or doing amiss, but also by doing things in themselves right which yet are not what God would have us do. We are strangely ingenious in perpetual self-seeking; and the things which worldly people do overtly, those who want to serve God sometimes do with more refinement, under some pretext which hides the faultiness of their conduct.

One general rule for the right use of time is to accustom yourself to live in continual dependence upon God's Holy Spirit, receiving whatever He vouchsafes to give from one moment to another, referring all doubts to Him, and, where an immediate course of action has to be taken, seeking strength in Him,—lifting up your heart to Him whenever you become aware that outward things are leading you away, or tending to forgetfulness or separation from God.

Blessed is that soul which by sincere self-renunciation abides always in its Creator's Hands, ready to do whatever He wills, not weary of saying a hundred times daily, "Lord, what wilt Thou have me to do? Teach me to do Thy Will, for Thou art my God. Send forth Thy Light, Lord, to guide me; teach me to use the present time to Thy service, forgive the misuse of what is past, and may I never blindly reckon on an uncertain future."

With respect to business and external duties, we only need for the right use of time to give a straightforward diligent heed to the ordering of God's Providence. As all such duties are the result of His plans, we have but to accept them dutifully, submitting our own tempers, fancies, inclinations, our self-will, our fastidiousness or restless anxiety, our hurry, in short all our own natural impulses to do what we like how we like. Take care not to let yourself be overwhelmed by outer things, nor utterly immersed in external interests, however important.

Every undertaking should be begun with a definite view to God's Glory, continued quietly, and ended without excitement or impatience.

The time spent in society and amusement is generally that most dangerous to one's self, though it may be very useful to others. Be on your guard, that is to say, be more faithful in remembering the Presence of God at such times. You need then especially to cultivate the watchfulness so often enjoined by our Lord,—to use aspirations and liftings up of your heart to Him, as the only Source of strength and safety; otherwise you can scarcely hope to be kept from the subtle venom so often lurking amid society and its pleasures, or to be really useful to others. This is more than ever necessary for those whose position carries great weight, and whose words may do so much good or so much harm.

Spare time is often the pleasantest and the most useful as concerns one's self; it can hardly find a better use than that of renewing our strength (and this bodily as well as mental) through secret communion with God. Prayer is so necessary, it is the source of so much blessing, that when once the soul has realised its gifts, it will hardly fail to seek them anew so often as it is free to do so.

CXXVI.

TO ONE LIVING IN THE WORLD. ON THE LAWFULNESS OF AMUSEMENTS.

I DO not think you need to trouble about those entertainments which you are inevitably called upon to share. Some people would fain always be grumbling and bemoaning themselves about the amusements in which they are obliged to take part; but for myself, I must say I do not at all sympathise with such unbending strictness. I like a much simpler line of conduct, and I believe such to be more acceptable to God. Where amusements are innocent in themselves and come in the ordinary way of things, according to the state of life to which God has called a person, I think it is enough if she shares in them moderately, and as in God's Sight. A stiff, constrained tone,—harsh, unbending, disobliging manners,—only tend to give worldly people a mistaken impression of religion, whereas they are quite sufficiently inclined already to misjudge it, and to think that God can only be served in a gloomy, dull life.

So I should say that God having placed you in a position where you are expected to join in whatever goes on, all you have to do is to be quiet, and not torment yourself with perpetual scruples as to the hidden motives which may creep unconsciously into one's heart. If one were to persist in perpetually sounding the depths of that heart, there would be no end to it, and while intending to seek God one would become absorbed in self by such continual perquisition. Go on rather with a simple heart in all peace and joy; such are the fruits of the Holy Spirit. He who does all, even the commonest things, as in God's Presence, is still working for God when what he does seems neither serious nor substantial work: always taking for granted, that is, that such trifling duties come to him in the order of God's Providence, and that he conforms to such an order as regards his worldly position in their fulfilment.

Most people, when setting about their reformation or conversion, are much more anxious to spend their lives in doing some difficult or unusual thing than to purify their intentions and to renounce self-will in the ordinary duties of their position; but this is a great mistake. Far better make less outward alteration as to actions, and more inward change in the heart which prompts them. Those who are leading a decent, well-ordered life need much more interior than exterior change when they seek to become more earnest Christians. God does not care for lip service, or bodily gestures, or outward ceremonies:

what He requires is a will no longer divided betwixt Him and any creature,—a will plastic in His Hands, asking nothing and refusing nothing, never under any possible excuse willing ought that He does not will.

Try always to have this simple will—this will so imbued with God's Will, wherever His Providence may lead you. Seek Him during the hours which seem so empty, and they will become full to you through His Grace. Even the most unprofitable amusements will become a kind of good works, if you enter into them merely because of social obligations, and in conformity with the ordering of God's Providence. There is no freer heart than that which God leads by this simple path. You will find yourself going on like a little child whose mother leads it by the hand, while it never questions whither they are going; you will be content to be bound or free, to talk or be silent; you will learn, when higher things are unseasonable, to talk cheerfully about mere trifles—to teach yourself what S. Francis de Sales calls "*joyeusetés*," and therein to please yourself while pleasing others.

Perhaps you will reply that you would rather be occupied in more solid, serious matters. Possibly; but God would not rather have it so for you, inasmuch as He appoints what you would not choose for yourself. Surely you know that His choice is best. Very likely you might find more satisfaction in those solid pursuits for which He has given you a taste; but it is precisely the satisfaction of that taste, however good and desirable in itself, which He sees fit to deny you. Even our virtues need the purification of those contradictions which God suffers to thwart us, the more to set us free from self-will. Nothing is so simple, gentle, loveable, discreet, and stedfast in every duty as real religion founded on dutiful acceptance of the Will of God, apart from personal tastes and likings, impetuosity and impulse. One so actuated leads very much the same life as all around, without affectation or strictness, sociable and easy in manner, but always regulated by duty, unremitting in giving up whatever is at discord with God's appointed way, looking stedfastly to God, and offering all the impulsive tendencies of natural disposition to Him. This is the real worship in spirit and in truth which Jesus Christ and the Father require. All else is mere formal religion, the shadow rather than the substance of Christianity.

Doubtless you will ask how you are to attain and to maintain such purity of intention amid so secular a life, one so devoted to mere amusement as yours seems to be. It is hard enough, you will say, to shield one's heart from the torrent of passion and bad worldly example with continual, absorbing self-watchfulness: how then can I hope to withstand, if I expose myself so readily to amusements which must defile, or at all events dangerously distract, a Christian's soul?

I acknowledge the danger; indeed, I hold it to be greater than words can express. I entirely agree as to the need for precaution amid so many snares; and these precautions I would sum up as follows:—

First, I would have you lay, as the foundation of all else, regular reading and prayer. I am not speaking of mere reading to satisfy intellectual cravings or theological controversy. Nothing could be more useless, unfitting, or dangerous for you. I mean plain reading, apart from all argument, confined to practical matters, and adapted to nourish the soul. Avoid all that excites your mind and lessens that blessed simplicity which renders it docile and submissive to the Church's teaching. If you read, not that you may be learned, but in order to know better how to mistrust self, your reading will be very profitable. Join prayer to your reading, and meditate on the great truths of religion. This you may do by fixing your attention on some act or words of Jesus Christ. Then, when penetrated with the truth you have been contemplating, apply it earnestly and closely to the correction of your own special faults; make resolutions before the Presence of God, and ask His Help, that you may fulfil that which He incites you to promise. When you find your attention wandering, recall it quietly, without being distressed;

and never let yourself be disheartened by the importunity of such distractions, which are very persistent. So long as they are involuntary, they cannot hurt you; on the contrary, they may help you more than life and sweetness in prayer, if they humble, mortify, and teach you to seek God for Himself alone, not for the pleasure found in the search. So long as you are stedfast in securing time, morning and evening, for these exercises, you will find that they will more than counterbalance the dangers which surround you. I say morning and evening, because just as the body requires regular support, so does the soul, to save it from becoming exhausted through constant contact with the world. So be firm both with yourself and others in always securing this time: never let yourself be led away by any engagements, however worthy they seem, to neglect taking this most needful food.

The second precaution I would recommend is to take, as often as you may be able and feel useful, certain days for complete retirement and recollection. This is a great means for healing all wounds at the Feet of Christ, and for counteracting the evil influences of the world. It will even promote your physical health, for if you use such brief retreats wisely, they will refresh your body as much as your mind.

Thirdly, I take it for granted that you limit yourself to such amusements as are not inconsistent with your profession of godliness, or with the good example which the world has a right to expect of you. For the world, in all its worldliness, expects those who hold it in contempt to be consistent in so doing ; and it cannot help respecting such as are stedfast and sincere in despising it. You can see that true Christians may well be thankful that the world is so severe a censor, inasmuch as that makes it most urgently incumbent on them never to give the least cause for scandal.

And, lastly, I think you should only take part in Court entertainments so far as your position calls you to do, or as due courtesy requires. Thus, when neither summoned nor invited, I would not have you join in them, nor ever seek invitations either directly or indirectly. By this means you will be able to give all the time at your own disposal to your household claims and to religious duties ; and the world, or at all events all sensible, unprejudiced people in it, will be edified when they see you at once gratefully accepting retirement when it is open to you and sociably entering into all lawful amusements when called upon to share them.

I am certain that, if you will comply with these simple rules, you will find an abundant blessing in them. God, Whose Hand seems to lead you into such scenes of pleasure, will uphold you in them. He will make Himself known to you, and the sweetness of His Presence will be far beyond that of all possible worldly pleasures. You will be moderate, discreet, and recollected,—free from constraint, affectation, or whatever else is unpleasant to others; you will be in the world without being of it, and your cheerful, kindly temper will make you all things to all men.

When you find that weariness depresses or amusement distracts you, you will calmly turn to the ever-ready Bosom of your Father without being discomposed. You will look to Him for gladness and refreshment when depressed, for moderation and recollection when distracted, and you will find that He will never leave you to want. A trustful glance, a silent movement of the heart towards Him, will renew your strength; and though you may often feel as if your soul was downcast and numb, whatever God calls you to do, He will give you power and courage to perform. This is the daily bread which we ask continually, and which will never fail us; for our Heavenly Father, so far from ever overlooking us, is always watching to find an open heart into which He may freely pour the torrents of His Grace.

CXXVII.

TO A LADY AT COURT. THE BURDEN OF PROSPERITY.

CHAINS of gold are no less chains than those of iron; and while the wearer is an object of envy she is worthy of compassion! Your captivity is noways preferable to that of one kept unjustly in prison,—the only real comfort is that it is God Who deprives you of liberty, and this is the same comfort by which the innocent prisoner above named would be upheld. So all you have more than such an one is a phantom of glory, which gives you no real advantage, but exposes you to the risk of being dazzled and deceived.

But, after all, the consolation of knowing that you are where you are through God's Providence is quite inexhaustible: while you have that, nothing can matter; and by it the iron chains are transformed, I will not say to gold—for we have just agreed that golden chains are nothing better!—but into liberty and happiness. What is the good of that natural liberty of which we are so jealous? It only sets us free to follow our own unruly inclinations even in things lawful; to indulge pride and presume on independence; to carry out our own will, which is the very worst thing that can happen to us. Well is it for those whom God cuts off from their own will that they may follow His, and woe indeed to such as are bound by their passions; they are just as miserable as the others are blessed. Bearing these bonds, the first cannot please themselves; from morning to night they do what God would have done, not what they like; so much the better: He holds them bound, so to say, hand and foot by His Will, He never leaves them a moment to themselves, He is jealous of that tyrannous "I" which wants everything its own way; He leads them on from one sacrifice to another, from one trouble to another, and trains them to fulfil His noblest plans amid commonplace annoyances, frivolous society, and trivialities of which they feel ashamed. He urges the faithful soul till it has scarce time to draw breath: no sooner has one interruption ceased than God sends another to carry on His Work. The soul would fain be free to think upon God, but all the while it is far more really united to Him by yielding to the cross He sends than by the most glowing, tender affections. He would fain be more his own in order to belong the more to God! he forgets that one never so little belongs to God as when self asserts its claim. That "I" by means of which we fancy we can unite ourselves to God, puts a wider gulf between Him and us than the most ridiculous frivolity, for there is a venom in self which does not exist in mere childish amusement.

Of course you should make use of all available moments to loosen your bonds, and specially try to secure certain hours for the refreshment of body and mind by recollection; but as to the rest of the day, if the stream carries you away in spite of yourself, you must yield without regret. You will learn to find God amid the stream of distractions, and that all the more really that it is not a self-chosen path.

The discomfort you feel in this subject state is natural weariness craving for ease rather than any leading of God's Holy Spirit. You fancy you are missing God, but it is self you really miss; for the most trying side of this exciting life of constraint is that you are never free as regards *yourself*. It is the lingering spirit of self which would like a quieter state of things in which to enjoy its own intellect and gifts, and to air all its good qualities in the society of a chosen few who would soothe its self-consciousness: or, perhaps, it makes you wish to enjoy the consolations of religion in peace, just when God wills to send nothing but disturbance and contradiction, the more to mould you to His Will.

Some He leads by bitter privations: as to you, He seems to lead you by overwhelming you with the enjoyment of empty prosperity; He makes your lot hard and difficult by dint of those very things which blind outsiders fancy to be the most perfect enjoyment of life! And so

He carries on two good works in you,—He teaches you by experience, and causes you to mortify self by the very things which foster evil and wickedness in many men. You are like that king we read of beneath whose hand whatever he touched turned to gold, and whose riches were his misery; but you can turn your worldly prosperity to a blessing by leaving all to God, not even seeking to find Himself save wherein He chooses to reveal Himself to you. As I was thinking of your troubles and the bondage of which you complain, our Lord's words to S. Peter came to my mind: "When thou wast young, thou girdedst thyself, and walkedst whither thou wouldest: but when thou shalt be old, thou shalt stretch forth thine hands, and another shall gird thee, and carry thee whither thou wouldest not."[1] Let yourself be carried; do not draw back. Like S. Peter you will be carried whither nature—keen after freedom and life—would fain not go,—you will be carried to the love of God, to perfect self-renunciation, to a thorough "death unto self" through God, Who works in you according to His Good Pleasure.

You must not wait for freedom and retirement to learn detachment; the prospect of such a time is very visionary,—it may never come: we must all be ready, should it so please God, to die in harness. If He forestalls our

[1] John xxi. 18.

plans for retirement, we are not our own, and He will only require of us that which it is in our power to give. The Israelites by the waters of Babylon longed sore after Jerusalem, yet how many were there not among them who never saw their beloved country again, but ended their lives in Babylon! How great would their delusion have been had they postponed a hearty, true service of God until they could once more see their native land! Ah, well! it may be that our lot will be like those Israelites!

CXXVIII.

TO A LADY AT COURT. GOD'S VARIOUS CROSSES.

GOD is very ingenious in making crosses for us. Some He makes of lead and iron, which are overwhelming in themselves; and some He makes of straw, which seem so light and yet are no less heavy to bear: others He makes of gold and jewels, the glitter of which dazzles those around and excites the world's envy, but which all the while are as crucifying as the most despised of crosses. He makes us crosses of whatever we love best, and turns all to bitterness. High position involves constraint and harass; it gives things we do not care for, and takes away the things we crave.

The poor man who has not bread to eat finds a leaden

cross in his poverty, and God mingles troubles very much akin to his with the cup of the prosperous. The rich man hungers for freedom and ease as the poor man hungers for bread; and whereas the latter can freely knock at every door and call upon every passer-by for pity, the man of high estate is ashamed[1] to seek compassion or relief. God very often adds bodily weakness to this moral servitude among the great; and nothing can be more profitable than two such crosses combined: they crucify a man from head to foot, and teach him his own lack of power and the uselessness of all he possesses. The world does not see your cross,—it only perceives some bondage softened by the possession of authority, and some slight indisposition which it probably attributes to fancy; while all the time you see nothing but bitterness, hardness, *ennui*, slavery, depression, pain, impatience! All that dazzles the distant spectator vanishes before the eyes of its possessor, whom God nails to the Cross, while all the world envies her!

So it is that Providence tries us in all manner of ways according to our position. Truly it is very possible to drink the cup of bitterness amid grandeur and without enduring calamity,—nay, to drink it to the very bitterest dregs out of the golden vessels which adorn the tables of kings! It is God's Good Pleasure thus to confound

[1] "pauvre honteux."

human greatness, which is really no more than disguised powerlessness. Happy they who see these things with that illumination of heart of which S. Paul speaks. You know by experience that Court favour can give no real happiness; it can do nothing to remedy the most ordinary natural sufferings, while it adds many more, and those sharp pangs enough, to what nature lays on us. The trials of high position are more acute than rheumatism or headache! But religion turns them all to good account; it teaches us to look upon all such things as a mere bondage, and in the patient acceptance thereof it shows us a real freedom, which is all the more real because it is hidden to the outer gaze.

No; the only good point of worldly prosperity is one to which the world is blind,—its cross! An elevated position does not save us from any of the ordinary afflictions common to men; indeed, it has its own special trials, and furthermore, it involves a bondage which prevents people from seeking the relief open to those in a less exalted place. They who are not in high place can at least, when ill, see whom they will, and be sheltered from outward disturbance; but the courtier must carry his whole cross; he must live for others when he would fain study his own comfort; he must put aside wants, feelings, wishes,—must admit nothing to be an inconvenience, and must submit to all the restraints of his too good fortune. It is thus that God turns the good things which the world covets into a trouble and toil—that He suffers those whom He has raised to earthly grandeur to be an example to others. It is His Will to perfect His Cross by concealing it beneath the most splendid worldly prosperity, in order to show its little value. Let me repeat it, happy they who in such circumstances learn to see God's Hand bruising them in mercy. Surely it is a blessed thing to find one's purgatory in that which to the worldly seems paradise, and in seeking which they too often forfeit the hope of a true Paradise after this brief life ends.

For those thus circumstanced there is not much to do. God does not need much speaking, or even much systematic thought; He sees the heart, and that is enough; He sees its suffering and its submission. We do not trouble ourselves to say perpetually to some beloved friend, "I love you with all my heart:" so it may easily chance that for a long time together we do not reflect upon our love for Him, and yet that meanwhile we love Him every whit as much as though we were making the fondest protestations. True love abides deep down in the heart, quietly, simply, silently. We do but stun ourselves with a multiplicity of fancies and talk; all such excitable love is but a work of the imagination.

In suffering, the only thing to be done is to suffer silently in God's Presence: "I became dumb, and opened not my mouth, for it was Thy doing."[1] Depression, illness, oppression of the brain, faintness, exhaustion, interruptions, restraints, all are sent by God. He gives you high position, with all its torments and wearisome surroundings; He sends the discouragement, the deadness, the impatience which accompany it, in order to humble you through temptation, and to show you to yourself in your true colours. All things are His doing; our part is to see and worship Him in them all. But do not harass yourself with trying to excite an artificial sense of God's Presence or of any such truths within yourself; far better is it to abide His time quietly with a submissive heart, or at most from time to time to make a quiet, calm act when your heart moves you thereto. By degrees you will learn that all the trouble of your position, your sufferings from bad health, and even your inward failings, are real antidotes to the poison of what in itself is a very perilous condition, so long as they are borne patiently and meekly. The one real treasure of great seeming prosperity is its hidden Cross. O Cross! Holy Cross! may I cleave to thee, may I worship my Lord as He hangs upon thee, and may I die with Him to sin and the world for ever!

[1] Ps. xxxix. 10.

CXXIX.

ON EXCESSIVE SENSITIVENESS TO TRIALS.

Your great sensitiveness does not depend upon yourself; God lets it form part of some people's natural temperament in order to train and discipline them, and then He sees fit not to remove it, but rather to use it for their sanctification. Their part is to enter into His views for them.

Temptations are inevitable and necessary to all; the question is how to avoid yielding to them. Inward temptations are like outward temptations in this, that in all victory will follow after a stedfast combat. Inward temptations are the most profitable, because they humble us most effectually, and teach us our own secret weakness. Outward temptations rather set forth the wickedness of the world around, while those assailing us within teach us that we are really as faulty as the world without. So bear your interior troubles and temptations in a spirit of humble trust and peace, just as you would try to bear the storms which assail you by means of your fellow-creatures. All come alike from God's Hands; He often uses us ourselves as well as others as instruments of our own discipline. Our pride grows restless and disheartened when it sees how full of inward rebellion our hearts are, because it would be so much pleasanter and more acceptable to find all our passions perfectly submissive, and to be able to look complacently at our own goodness. You must try to have a stedfast will, in spite of revulsions and natural excitement, and be patient when it pleases God to show you by such storms to what perils of shipwreck you are exposed, unless His all-powerful Hand preserves you. And should you ever unhappily fall into some voluntary imperfections, humble yourself, prostrate yourself, correct yourself unsparingly, do not lose an instant in retracing your steps towards God, but do it all unaffectedly and quietly. Rise up and begin again vigorously, without yielding to mortification and discouragement because of your fall.

CXXX.

GOD'S SEVERITY ALL LOVE.

STRICT as God seems to you in His dealings with souls, He never inflicts any suffering solely to give pain; He always has their purification in view. The severity of the operation is caused by the depth of the malady to be cured; God would not cut were there no sore,—He only probes the ulcerated proud flesh. So, after all, it is our own noxious self-will which is the cause of what we suffer, and God's Hand deals as gently with us as may be. But how deep, how malignant our souls must be, since all the time He is sparing us so tenderly He yet puts us to such grievous pain!

Again, just as God only wounds for our healing, so He never deprives us of any of His gifts, save to restore them a hundredfold. In His Love He takes away even His purest gifts if we are using them amiss; and the purer those gifts the more jealous He is that we should not reckon upon them as our own, or take credit to ourselves for them. The most eminent graces turn to deadly poison if we rest upon them in self-complacent security. This was the sin of the fallen angels; so soon as they looked upon their exalted state as their own assured possession they became the enemies of God, and were driven forth from His Kingdom.

We may learn from this how little men understand about the real nature of sin. This is the greatest of all sins, yet there are but few souls so pure as to enjoy God's gifts without any intermixture of selfish complacency. In thinking of God's graces, self is almost always uppermost: we are troubled when we realise our own weakness; we take delight in conscious strength; we seldom weigh our own perfection solely with a view to God's Glory, as we might do that of another person; we are saddened and depressed when sensible sweetness and conscious grace forsake us; in short, we are almost always thinking, not of God, but of self. And so all our good things need purifying, lest they foster a merely natural life in us. Our corrupt nature finds a very subtle food in the graces which are most opposed to nature; self-love is fed, not merely by humiliations and austerities, by fervent prayer and mortification, but even by the fullest self-renunciation and utter sacrifice. There is an infinite amount of moral stay in the thought that we have no stay at all, and that amid such a horrible trial we are still yielding ourselves up unreservedly. And so, to make the sacrifice real, we need that it too be consumed on the altar,—we must give up even our satisfaction in that sacrifice.

The only way to find God truly is in this readiness to part with all His gifts, this thorough sacrifice of self, and of all inward resource. God's exceeding jealousy exacts it, and you can easily see how we never lose ourselves in Him until all else fails us. A man who is falling into an abyss is not wholly precipitated so long as he can clutch hold of the sides. And self-love, even when God overthrows it, clutches in its despair at every gleam of hope, like a drowning man grasping at the reeds around.

You must learn to realise the necessity of this deprivation of all God's gifts, which He gradually works out. There is no one gift, however precious, which, after having been a help, will not become a snare and a hindrance to the soul which rests in it; and so God often takes away that which He had given. Not, however, wholly; He often deprives us of something only in order to restore it more fully, and without the evil spirit of self-satisfaction which had unconsciously got possession of us. This is overthrown by the loss, and then He restores it a hundredfold. And then the soul loses sight of the gift and sees God only.

CXXXI.

CHRISTIAN PERFECTION.

CHRISTIAN perfection is not the strict, wearisome, constrained thing you suppose. It requires a person to give himself to God with his whole heart, and so soon as this is accomplished, whatever he is called upon to do for God becomes easy. Those who are wholly God's are always satisfied, for they desire only that which He wills, and are ready to do whatever He requires; they are ready to strip themselves of all things, and are sure to find a hundredfold in that nakedness. This hundredfold happiness which the true children of God possess amid all the troubles of this world consists in a peaceful conscience, freedom of spirit, a welcome resignation of all things to God, the joyful sense of His Light ever waxing stronger within their heart, and a thorough deliverance from all tyrannous fears and longings after worldly things. They make sacrifices, but for Him they love best; they suffer, but willingly, and realising such suffering to be better than any worldly joy; their body may be diseased, their mind languid and shrinking, but their will is firm and stedfast, and they can say a hearty *Amen* to every blow which it pleases God to deal them.

What God requires is an undivided will—a yielding will, desiring only what He desires, rejecting only what He rejects, and both unreservedly. Where such a mind is everything turns to good, and its very amusements become good works. Happy indeed is such an one! he is delivered from all his own passions,—from the judgments of men, their unkindness, their slavish maxims, their cold, heartless mockery; from the troubles of what the world calls fortune; from the treachery or forgetfulness of friends, the snares of enemies, his own weakness; from the weariness of this brief life, the terrors of an unholy death, the bitter remorse which follows sin, and from the eternal condemnation of God. From all these endless evils the Christian is set free; he has resigned his will to God and knows no will save His, and thus faith and hope are his comfort amid all possible sorrows. Is it not a grievous mistake to be afraid to give yourself to God and to commit yourself to so blessed a state of things? Blessed are they who throw themselves headlong and blindfold into the Arms of "the

Father of all Mercies and God of all Comfort."[1] Nothing remains for them save to know Him better and better; no fear, save lest they be not quick enough to see what He requires. Directly that they discover any fresh light from His Law, they "rejoice as one that findeth a hid treasure." Let what may befall the true Christian, all is well to his mind; he only seeks to love God more, and the further he learns to tread in the way of perfection the lighter he feels his yoke.

Cannot you see that it is mere folly to be afraid of giving yourself too entirely to God? It merely means that you are afraid of being too happy, of accepting His Will in all things too heartily, of bearing your inevitable trials too bravely, of finding too much rest in His Love, and of sitting too loosely to the worldly passions which make you miserable. Try to despise all that is of the world that you may be wholly God's. I do not say that you should cut yourself off from all earthly affections; to one like yourself, who is leading a good, well-regulated life, all that is needed is that the motive power become that of Love. You would then do very much the same things that you do now, for God does not alter the condition He has assigned to each or the duties appertaining thereto: the alteration would be that, whereas now you fulfil your duties for your own satisfaction and that of

[1] 2 Cor. i. 3.

the world around, you would then pursue the same line as now; but instead of being eaten up by pride or passion—instead of living in bondage to the world's malicious criticism—you would act freely and bravely in the fulness of hope in God,—you would be full of trust, and looking forward to eternal blessings would comfort you for the earthly happiness which seems to slip from under your feet; God's Love would give wings to your feet in treading His paths and lifting you up beyond all your cares. If you doubt me, try: "O taste and see how gracious the Lord is!"

The Son of God says to all Christians without any exception, "If any man will come after Me, let him take up his cross and follow Me."[1] The broad road leads to destruction; strive to follow that narrow path on which so few enter. Only the "violent take the Kingdom of Heaven by storm." You must be born anew, renounce and despise yourself, become as a little child, mourn that you may be comforted, and not be of this world, which is condemned because of unbelief.

These truths frighten many, and that because they only see what religion requires without realising what it offers, or the loving spirit by which it makes every burthen light. They do not understand that such religion leads a person to the very highest perfection by

[1] Matt. xvi. 24.

filling him with a loving peace which lightens every woe. Those who have given themselves unreservedly to God are always happy. They realise that the yoke of Jesus Christ is light and easy, that in Him they do indeed find rest, and that He lightens the load of all that are weary and heavy laden, as He promised. But what can be more wretched than those hesitating, cowardly souls which are divided between God and the world. They will and will not; they are torn asunder both by their own passions and by remorse at their indulgence; they are alike afraid of God's judgments and those of men; they are afraid of what is evil and ashamed of what is good; they have all the trials of goodness without its comfort! If they had but the courage to despise idle talk, petty ridicule, and the rash judgments of men, what peace and rest they might enjoy in the Bosom of God!

Nothing is more perilous to your own salvation, more unworthy of God, or more hurtful to your ordinary happiness, than being content to abide as you are. Our whole life is given us with the object of going boldly on towards the Heavenly Home. The world slips away like a deceitful shadow, and eternity draws near; why delay to push forward? While it is time, while your Merciful Father lights up your path, make haste and seek His Kingdom.

The first Commandment of the Law alone is enough to banish all excuse for any reserve with God: "Thou shalt love the Lord thy God with all thy heart, and with all thy soul, and with all thy strength, and with all thy mind."[1] Observe how our Lord heaped together expressions which would forestall all the soul's evasions and reservations as regards God's jealous Love, requiring not merely the heart's strength and power, but that of the mind and thought. Who can deceive himself by thinking he loves God if he does not willingly ponder His Law, or try diligently to fulfil His holy Will? Be sure that all those who are reluctant to perceive fully what His Love requires are yet a long way off from it. There is but one true way of loving God, *i.e.* to do nothing save with and for Him, and to obey His every call with a "free spirit." Those who aim at a compromise, who would fain hold on to the world with one hand, cannot believe this, and so they run the risk of being among those "lukewarm" whom God will reject.[2]

Surely those cowardly souls which say, "Thus far will I go, but no farther," must be most displeasing to God. Does it beseem the clay to dictate to the potter? What would men of the world think of a servant or a subject who presumed to offer such a half-service to his master or monarch, who shrank from a too hearty fulfilment of

[1] Luke x. 27.   [2] Rev. iii. 16.

his duty, and was ashamed to let his loyalty be seen? And if so, what will the King of Kings say if we pursue such cowardly conduct? The time is at hand, He will soon come; let us prevent Him, let us adore that eternal beauty which never grows old, and which imparts perpetual youth to such as love none else. Let us turn from this miserable world, which is already beginning to crumble away. How many great people we have lately seen pass away beneath the cold hand of Death! We shall soon be called to leave this world we love so dearly, and which is nought save vanity, weakness, and folly,—a mere shadow passing away.

CXXXII.

SIMPLICITY AND SELF-CONSCIOUSNESS.

THERE is a simplicity which is merely a fault, and there is a simplicity which is a wonderful virtue. Sometimes it comes from a want of perception, and ignorance of what is due to others. In the world when people call any one simple they generally mean a foolish, ignorant, credulous person. But real simplicity, so far from being foolish, is almost sublime. All good men like and admire it, are conscious of sinning against it, observe it in others, and know what it involves, and yet they could not precisely define it. One may apply to it what is said in the *Imitation* of compunction of heart: " I would rather feel it than know how to define it."[1]

I should say that simplicity is an uprightness of soul which prevents self-consciousness. It is not the same as sincerity, which is a much humbler virtue. Many people are sincere who are not simple;—they say nothing but what they believe to be true, and do not aim at appearing anything but what they are; but they are continually in fear of passing for something they are not; and so they are for ever thinking about themselves, weighing their every word and thought, and dwelling upon themselves, in apprehension of having done too much or too little. These people are sincere, but they are not simple; they are not at their ease with others, or others with them; there is nothing easy, frank, unrestrained, or natural about them: one feels one would like less admirable people better, who were not so stiff. This is how men feel, and God's judgment is the same; He does not like souls which are self-absorbed and always, so to say, looking at themselves in a mirror.

To be absorbed in the world around, and never turn a thought within, as is the blind condition of some who are carried away by what is present and tangible, is one extreme as opposed to simplicity. And to be self-absorbed in everything, whether it be duty to God or

[1] Book I. c. i. 3.

man, is the other extreme, which makes a person wise in his own conceits,—reserved, self-conscious, uneasy at the least thing which disturbs his inward self-complacency. Such false wisdom, in spite of its solemnity, is hardly less vain and foolish than the folly of those who plunge headlong into worldly pleasure. The one is intoxicated by his outer surroundings, the other by what he believes himself to be doing inwardly; but both are in a state of intoxication, and the last is a worse state than the first, because it seems to be wise, though it is not really, and so people do not try to be cured;—they rather pride themselves on it, and feel exalted above others by it. It is a sickness somewhat like insanity;—a man may be at death's door while affirming himself to be well.

He who is so carried away by outer things that he never looks within is in a state of worldly intoxication; and he who dissects himself continually becomes affected, and is equally far from being simple.

Real simplicity lies in a *juste milieu*, equally free from thoughtlessness and affectation, in which the soul is not overwhelmed by externals so as to be unable to reflect, nor yet given up to the endless refinements which self-consciousness induces. That soul which looks where it is going, without losing time arguing over every step, or looking back perpetually, possesses true simplicity.

The first step, then, is for the soul so to put away outward things and look within as to know its own real interests; so far all is right and natural; thus much is only a wise self-love which seeks to avoid the intoxication of the world.

In the next step the soul must add the contemplation of God, Whom it fears, to that of self. This is a faint approach to real wisdom, but the soul is still greatly self-absorbed: it is not satisfied with fearing God; it wants to be certain that it does fear Him, and fears lest it fear Him not, going round in a perpetual circle of self-consciousness. All this restless dwelling in self is very far from the peace and freedom of real love; but that is yet in the distance,—the soul must needs go through a season of trial, and were it suddenly plunged into a state of rest, it would not know how to use it.

The first man fell through self-indulgence, and his descendants have to go through much the same course, gradually coming from out self to seek God. For a while, then, it is well to let the penitent soul struggle with itself and its faults, before attaining the freedom of the children of God. But when God begins to open the heart to something higher and purer, then is the time to follow on the workings of His power step by step; and so the soul attains true simplicity.

The third step is that, ceasing from a restless self-contemplation, the soul begins to dwell upon God instead, and by degrees forgets itself in Him,—it becomes full of Him and ceases to feed upon self. Such a soul is not blinded to its own faults or indifferent to its own errors; it is more conscious of them than ever, and increased light shows them in plainer form, but this self-knowledge comes from God, and therefore it is not restless or uneasy.

Much anxious contemplation of our own faults hinders the soul as a traveller is hindered by an excessive quantity of cumbrous wraps, which prevent his walking freely. Superstition and scruples, and even, contrary as it seems at first sight, presumption, readily grow out of such self-consuming processes. Real Christian simplicity is generous and upright, and forgets itself in unreserved resignation to God. If we men expect our earthly friends to be free and open-hearted with us, how much more will God, our best Friend, require a single-hearted, open, unreserved intercourse? Such simplicity is the perfection of God's true children, the object at which we should all aim. The greatest hindrance to its attainment is the false wisdom of the world, which fears to trust anything to God,—which wants to achieve everything by its own skill, to settle everything its own way, and indulge in ceaseless self-admiration. This is the wisdom of the world which, S. Paul tells us, is foolishness with God;[1]

[1] 1 Cor. iii. 19.

whereas true wisdom, which lies in yielding one's self up unreservedly to God's Holy Spirit, is mere foolishness in the world's eyes.

In the first stages of conversion we are forced continually to urge wisdom upon the Christian; when he is thoroughly converted, we have to fear lest he be wise overmuch, and it is needful to warn him that he "think soberly," as S. Paul says :[1] and when at last he craves a nearer approach to God, He must needs lose himself, to find himself again in God; he must lay aside that worldly wisdom which is so great a stay to self-reliant natures, he must drain the bitter cup of the "foolishness of the Cross," which has so often been the substitute for martyrdom with those who are not called on to shed their blood like the primitive Christians. When once all self-seeking and brooding is overcome, the soul acquires indescribable peace and freedom :—we may write about it, but only experience can really teach any one what it is. The person who attains it is like a child at its mother's breast, free from fears or longings, ready to be turned hither or thither, indifferent as to what others may think, save so far as charity always would shun scandal; always doing everything as well as possible, cheerfully, heartily, but regardless of success or failure. Such a person embodies S. Paul's words : "It is a very small thing that I

[1] Rom. xii. 3.

should be judged of man's judgment, yea, I judge not mine own self."[1]

But how far most of us are from this real simplicity of heart! Still the farther we are the more urgently we should seek it. Yet so far from being simple, the greater number of Christians are not even sincere. They are not merely artificial, but often false and dissimulating towards their neighbours, towards God, and towards themselves. What endless little manœuvres and unrealities and inventions people employ to distort truth! Alas, "all men are liars!"[2] even those who are naturally upright and sincere, whose temper is what we call frank and simple, are often jealously self-conscious, and foster a pride destroying all real simplicity which consists in genuine self-renunciation and forgetfulness of self.

But, you will ask, how can I help being constantly self-engrossed when a crowd of anxious thoughts disturb me and set me ill at ease? I only ask that which is in your own power. Never voluntarily give way to these disturbing anxieties. If you are stedfast in resisting them whenever you become conscious of their existence, by degrees you will get free, but do not hunt them out with the notion of conquering them;—do not seek a collision,—you will only feed the evil. A continual attempt to repress thoughts of self and self-interest is

[1] Cor. iv. 3.   [2] Ps. cxvi. 10.

practically continual self-consciousness, which will only distract you from the duties incumbent on you and deprive you of the sense of God's Presence.

The great thing is to resign all your interests and pleasures and comfort and fame to God. He who unreservedly accepts whatever God may give him in this world—humiliation, trouble, and trial from within or from without—has made a great step towards self-victory; he will not dread praise or censure, he will not be sensitive; or if he finds himself wincing, he will deal so cavalierly with his sensitiveness that it will soon die away. Such full resignation and unfeigned acquiescence is true liberty, and hence arises perfect simplicity. The soul which knows no self-seeking, no interested ends, is thoroughly candid; it goes on straight forward without hindrance, its path opens daily more and more to " perfect day," and its peace, amid whatever troubles beset it, will be as boundless as the depths of the sea. But the soul which still seeks self is constrained, hesitating, smothered by the risings of self-love. Blessed indeed are they who are no longer their own, but have given themselves wholly to God!

I have noticed to you before now how entirely the world takes the same view as God in this respect of a noble self-forgetting simplicity. The world knows how to appreciate among its own worldlings the easy, simple manners of unselfishness, and that because there is really nothing more beautiful and attractive than a thorough absence of self-consciousness. But this is out of keeping among worldly people, who rarely forget self unless it be when they are altogether absorbed by still more worthless external interests; yet even such simplicity of heart as the world can produce gives us some faint idea of the beauty of the real thing. They who cannot find the substance sometimes run after the shadow; and shadow though it be, it attracts them for want of better things.

Take a person full of faults, but not seeking to hide them, not attempting to shine, affecting neither talent, goodness, nor grace, not seeming to think more of himself than of others, not continually remembering that "I" to which we are most of us so alive; such a person will be generally liked in spite of many faults. His spurious simplicity passes as genuine. On the contrary, a very clever person, full of acquired virtues and external gifts, will always be jarring, disagreeable, and repulsive if he seems living in perpetual self-consciousness and affectation. So that we may safely say, that even from the lower point of view nothing is more attractive or desirable than a simple character free from self-consciousness.

But, you will say, am I never to think of myself, or of

what affects me, and never to speak of myself? No, indeed; I would not have you so constrained; such an attempt at being simple would destroy all simplicity. What is to be done, then? Make no rules at all, but try to avoid all affectation. When you are disposed to talk about yourself from self-consciousness, thwart the itching desire by quietly turning your attention to God, or to some duty He sets before you.

And remember, simplicity is free from false shame and mock modesty, as well as from ostentation and self-conceit. When you feel inclined to talk about yourself from vanity, the only thing to be done is to stop short as soon as may be; but if, on the other hand, there is some real reason for doing so, then do not perplex yourself with arguments, but go straight to the point. "But what will people think of me?" do you say? "I shall seem to be boasting foolishly, to be putting myself forward!" All such anxious thoughts are not worthy of a moment's attention; learn to speak frankly and simply of yourself as of others when it is necessary, just as S. Paul often speaks of himself in his Epistles. He alludes to his birth,[1] to his Roman citizenship;[2] he says that he was not "a whit behind the chiefest Apostles;"[3] that he had done even more than they all;[4] that "he withstood

---

[1] Acts xxi. 39. [2] Acts xxii. 28. [3] 2 Cor. xi. 5.
[4] 2 Cor. xi. 23.

Peter to the face because he was to be blamed;"[1] that he had "been caught up into Paradise, and heard unspeakable words;"[2] that he had "always a conscience void of offence toward God and toward men;"[3] that he "laboured more abundantly than they all:"[4] he bids the faithful "Be ye followers of me, even as I also am of Christ."[5] See with what dignity and simplicity he always speaks of himself, and is able to say even the loftiest things without displaying any emotion or self-consciousness. He describes what concerns himself just as he would describe something that had happened a thousand years ago. I do not mean that we can or ought all to do the same, but what I do mean is that whenever it is right to speak concerning one's self, it should be done simply. Of course, every one cannot attain S. Paul's sublime simplicity, and it were dangerous indeed to affect it; but when there is any real call to speak about yourself in ordinary life, try to do so in all straightforwardness, neither yielding to mock modesty nor to the shamefacedness which belongs to false pride, for indeed false pride often lurks behind a seemingly modest, reserved manner. We don't want to show off our own good points exactly; but we are very glad to let others find them out, so as to get double credit both for our virtues and our modesty in concealing them.

[1] Gal. ii. 11.   [2] 2 Cor. xii. 4.   [3] Acts xxiv. 16.
[4] 1 Cor. xv. 10.   [5] 1 Cor. xi. 1.

If you want to know how far you are really called upon to think or speak of yourself, consult some one who knows you thoroughly; by so doing you will avoid self-opinionated decisions, which it is always a great thing to do. A wise spiritual guide will be much more impartial than we can ever be towards ourselves in judging how far we are justified in bringing forward our own good deeds; and as for unforeseen occasions rising up suddenly, all you can do is to look to God for immediate guidance, and do unhesitatingly what He seems to indicate. You must act promptly, and even should you be wrong, He will accept your right intention if you have sought with a single heart to do what you believed to be right in His Eyes.

As to speaking of one's self in condemnation I can say little. If a person does so in real simplicity, through a sense of abhorrence and contempt of self inspired by God, the results have been very marvellous among saints. But ordinarily for us who are not saints, the safest course is never to speak of one's self, either good or bad, needlessly. Self-love would rather find fault with itself than abide silent and ignored. As to your faults, you should be watchful to correct them. There are many ways of doing this, but as a rule nothing is more helpful in the attempt than a spirit of recollection, a habit of checking eager longings and impulses, and entire resignation of yourself into God's Hand without a constant fretting self-inspection. When God undertakes the work, and we do not frustrate Him, it goes on apace.

Such simplicity as this influences all things, outward manner included, and makes people natural and unaffected. You get accustomed to act in a straightforward way, which is incomprehensible to those who are always self-occupied and artificial. Then even your faults will turn to good, humbling without depressing you. When God intends to make use of you for His Glory, either He will take away your failings or overrule them to His own ends, or at all events so order things that they should not be a stumbling-block to those among whom He sends you. And practically, those who attain such real inward simplicity generally acquire with it an ingenuous, natural outward manner, which may even sometimes appear somewhat too easy and careless, but which will be characterised by a truthful, gentle, innocent, cheerful, and calm simplicity, which is exceedingly attractive.

Verily such simplicity is a great treasure! How shall we attain to it? I would give all I possess for it; it is the costly pearl of Holy Scripture.[1] Worldly wisdom despises it, and oh, how it despises the world! But the carnal mind is enmity against God, and "they that are

[1] Matt. xiii. 46.

after the flesh do mind the things of the flesh; and they that are after the Spirit the things of the Spirit."[1]

CXXXIII.

ON THE PRESENCE OF GOD.

THE real mainspring of all perfection you will find contained in the precept given of old by God to Abraham: "Walk before Me, and be thou perfect."[2] The Presence of God will calm your spirit,—it will give you peaceful nights, and tranquillise your mind even amid the hardest day's work; but then for this you must give yourself up unreservedly to God. When once you have found God, you will realise that you need not to seek anything more among men; you must be ready to sacrifice even your dearest friendships, for the best of Friends is the Indweller of hearts. He is as a jealous bridegroom, who will tolerate no rival near him.

You do not need much time to love God, to renew the thought of His Presence frequently, to lift up your heart to Him and worship Him in its depths, to offer Him all you do and all you suffer; and this is the real "Kingdom of God within you,"[3] which nothing can disturb. If outward distractions and your own lively imagination hinder your soul from conscious recollection,

[1] Rom. viii. 5.   [2] Gen. xvii. 1.   [3] Luke xvii. 21.

at all events you must practise it in will; so doing the desire for recollectedness will become in itself a kind of recollection which will avail, especially if you turn resolutely towards God and do whatever He requires of you with a stedfast intention. Try at intervals to kindle within yourself a hearty desire to give yourself to God to the fullest extent of all your powers; your mind to know and think upon Him, and your will to love Him; and endeavour likewise to consecrate all your external actions to Him. Be on your guard not to let yourself be engrossed too entirely, or for any great length of time, with anything external or interior, the tendency of which is so to distract your heart and mind as to make it difficult for you to turn fully towards God.

The moment you feel that any extraneous object causes you overmuch pleasure or delight, sever your heart from it, and lest you should stop short in the creature, turn yourself at once to your only true End and Sovereign Good, God Himself. If you are stedfast in breaking off all creature-worship, and in reserving to God only that love and reverence which He requires, you will soon experience that true happiness which He never fails to give to the soul which sits loose to all earthly affections. When you are conscious that you are longing very earnestly for anything whatsoever, or that you are keenly excited about anything in which you are engaged, be it great or small, try to pause, and repress the eagerness of your thoughts and the excitement with which you are acting, and remember that God Himself tells us His Holy Spirit is not to be found in the storm or the whirlwind. Be watchful not to throw yourself too actively into all that is going on, nor let yourself become engrossed by it; for this is one great source of distractions. Directly that you have ascertained what the Lord would have you to do in each matter as it arises, stop there, and give no heed to all the rest. So doing you will be able to keep your mind calm and composed, and to shake off an infinity of useless matters which hamper the soul and hinder it from turning fully to God.

One excellent method of maintaining inward calmness and freedom is to keep putting aside all useless reflections on the past, whether of regret or self-complacency, and when one duty is accomplished, to go steadily on with the next,—confining your attention entirely to the one thing God gives you to do, and not forestalling difficulties for the future any more than regrets for the past. And again, accustom yourself to make a frequent brief act of God's Presence through the day, and amid all your occupations; whenever you are conscious that anxiety or disturbance are springing up within, calm yourself thus: sever yourself from all that is not of God; cut short useless thoughts and broodings; avoid unprofitable talk. If you seek for God within your heart, you will infallibly find Him, and with Him peace and happiness. As to your active occupations, try even in those to let God have the largest share. If you would fulfil your commonest duties well, you must do them as in His Presence, and for His Sake. The sight of His Majesty and Love will calm and strengthen you. A word from the Lord stilled the raging of the sea,[1] and a glance from us to Him, and from Him to us, will do the same in our daily life. Lift up your heart continually to God; He will purify, enlighten, and direct it. Try to be able to say with the holy king David, "I have set God always before me;"[2] and again: "Whom have I in heaven but Thee, and there is none upon earth that I desire in comparison of Thee. . . . Thou art the strength of my heart, and my portion for ever."[3] Do not wait till you can be alone to seek a recollected mind; the moment you become conscious of having lost recollection, strive to renew it. Turn to God simply, familiarly, trustfully. This can be done even amid the greatest interruptions as well as not, even when you are wearied and pestered with uncongenial society. All things, be sure, "work together for good to those that love God."[4]

You must be regular with such spiritual reading as is

---

[1] Mark vi. [2] Ps. xvi. 9. [3] Ps. lxxiii. 24, 25.
[4] Rom. viii. 28.

suited to your needs, making frequent pauses to hearken to the voice which will help to call your inner self to recollection. A very few words thus studied are a true manna to the soul. You may forget the actual words, but they are taking root all the time secretly, and your soul will feed upon them and be strengthened.

CXXXIV.

ON CONFORMITY TO THE WILL OF GOD.

You will find several chapters in the *Imitation* on Conformity to God's Will, which are marvellous, and also a great deal most helpful in S. Francis de Sales. The whole gist of the matter lies in the will, and this is what our Dear Lord meant by saying, "the Kingdom of God is within you."[1] It is not a question of how much we know, how clever we are, nor even how good; it all depends upon the heart's love. External actions are the results of love, the fruit it bears; but the source, the root, is in the deep of the heart. Some virtues are suitable to one condition in life, some to another; some to one season, some to another; but a hearty will we need at all seasons and in all places.

That Kingdom of God within us consists in always willing whatever God wills, wholly, unreservedly. It is

[1] Luke xvii. 21.

thus that our prayer "Thy Kingdom come" is fulfilled; thus that "His Will is done in earth as in Heaven;" thus that we become, so to say, identified with Him. Blessed are the poor in spirit! Blessed are they who strip themselves of all they can call their own, even their will; for this it is to be truly poor in spirit.

But how, you ask, are you to acquire this saintly will? By absolute conformity to that of God; by willing what He wills and desiring nothing which He does not will; by nailing, so to say, your feeble will to His All-powerful Will. If you do this, nothing can happen which you do not will, for nothing can happen save that which God orders; and you will find unfailing comfort and rest in submitting to His Will and Pleasure. Such a life within is indeed a foretaste of the blessedness of the saints, and their everlasting song, Amen, Alleluia!

As you learn to worship, praise, and bless God for all things,—to see His Hand everywhere,—you will feel nothing to be an unbearable evil; for everything, even the most cruel sufferings, will "turn to good" for you. Who would call *evil* the sorrows which God lays on him with a view to purify and make him meet for Himself? Surely what works out such exceeding good cannot be an evil? Cast all your cares into the Bosom of your Loving Father. Let Him do as He sees fit with you. Be content to obey His Will in all things, and to merge your will concerning everything in His. What right have you, who are not your own, to any intrinsic possession? A slave has no proprietary rights, how much less the creature which in itself is mere sin and nothingness, and which can possess nought save by the gift of God? God has endowed it with freewill in order that it may have somewhat real to offer Him. We have nothing to call our own save our will,—nothing else is ours. Sickness takes away health and life; riches melt away; mental powers depend upon a man's bodily strength;—the one only thing really ours is our will; and consequently, it is of this that God is jealous, for He gave it, not that we should use it as our own, but that we might restore it to Him, wholly and undividedly. Whoever holds back any particle of reluctance or desire as his right defrauds His Maker, to Whom all is due.

Alas! how many self-asserting souls we meet,—people who would fain do right and love God, but only after their own fashion and choice,—who practically lay down the law to God as to His dealings with them! They wish to serve Him and possess Him, but they will not give themselves up to Him and let Him possess them; and as a natural result, how much resistance God meets with from such people, even when they seem full of zeal and ardour for His service! To a certain degree, indeed, their spiritual abundance becomes a hindrance, because they look upon it as their own, and self-assertion mingles in their best works. Verily, the soul which is utterly impoverished, utterly devoid of self-existence, incapable of willing aught from hour to hour save that which God sets before it in the precepts of His Gospel and the ordering of His Providence, is far ahead of all those fervid enlightened people who persist in travelling to Heaven by their own self-chosen path.

This is the real meaning of those words of Jesus Christ: "If any man will come after Me, let him deny himself, and take up his cross, and follow Me."[1] We must *follow* Him step by step, not strike out a new road of our own by which to teach Him. He can only be followed by "denying" self. And what is it to deny self but to renounce all rights over self? Even as S. Paul says: "Ye are not your own."[2] Woe to those who take back the gift when once it is made.

Pray to the Father of Mercies, the God of Consolation, that He would tear out all that is of self in you, leaving no remnant behind. So painful an operation must be hard to bear; it is very difficult to lie still under God's Hand while He cuts to the quick; but this is the patience of Saints, the offering of pure faith. Let God do as He will with you. Never resist Him voluntarily even for a moment. The instant you become conscious

[1] Matt. xvi. 24.   [2] 1 Cor. vi. 19.

of the revulsion of nature and inclination, turn trustfully to Him, take His side against your own rebellious nature, give it up to God's Holy Spirit, and ask Him to put it by degrees to death. Watch, as in His Sight, over your most trifling faults; strive never to grieve the Holy Spirit, Who is so jealous over your hidden life. Make use of past faults to attain a humble consciousness of your own weakness, only without weariness or discouragement.

How could you give more glory to God than by absolutely setting aside self and all its longings, and letting Him send you where He pleases? It is thus that He will be your God, that His Kingdom will come in you, if independently of all outward hindrances and helps you look to nothing, within or without, save God's Hand overruling all things, your one unfailing worship.

If you persist in serving Him in one place or one way rather than another, you are serving Him according to your will, not His; but if you are ready to go anywhere and do anything, if you leave yourself to be entirely moulded by His Providence, putting no limits to your submission, this is indeed taking up your Cross and following Him. Then you would be perfectly happy if He were to lay the heaviest trials on you for His great Glory.

Open your heart wide, unboundedly wide, and let God's Love flow in as a torrent. Fear nothing on your way; God will lead you by the hand, if only you trust Him wholly, and are filled rather with love for Him than fear for yourself.

CXXXV.

INWARD PEACE.

There can never be peace for those who resist God. Whatever real happiness there is to be found in this world is reserved for the pure conscience;—the whole earth is a place of tribulation and anguish for the evil conscience. What a different thing God's Peace is from that which the world affects to give! It stills the passions, preserves the conscience pure and just, draws us to God, strengthens us against temptation. This purity of conscience is preserved by constantly frequenting the Sacraments: temptation, when it does not prevail, always does its work. The peace of which I speak lies in thorough resignation to God's Will.

"Martha, Martha, thou art troubled about many things: but one thing is needful." The needful to you is a simple heart, that quiet spirit which results from absolute resignation to whatever God appoints, the patience and toleration for your neighbour's faults which a sense of God's Presence teaches; frankness and childlike simplicity in acknowledging your faults, and accepting reproof and counsel; these are the solid graces which are needful for your sanctification. The anxiety you feel about so many things only comes from your not heartily accepting whatever befalls you, as coming from God's Hand. Leave everything to Him, and forestall whatever may happen by offering it all to Him. The very moment you cease to want things to be according to your own judgment, and accept unconditionally whatever He sends, you will be delivered from all the retrospects and forebodings and hesitations which harass you. There will no longer be anything to hide, or to bring about. But till then, you will be perplexed, changeable in your views and tastes, easily displeased with others, out of harmony with yourself, full of reserve and mistrust; your good sense, until it becomes humble and simple, will only tend to trouble you; your devotion, albeit sincere, will serve less to sustain and comfort you than to fill you with inward self-reproach. But if, on the contrary, you give yourself up heartily to God, you will be at rest, and filled with the holy joy of His gracious Spirit.

Beware of looking to man in what is God's Work alone. In the matter of guidance, reckon all human beings as nought: the slightest tinge of human respect dries up the source of grace, and will add to your irresolution; you will suffer greatly, and offend yet more against God.

How should you not give your whole heart to God,

Who loved you before you loved Him, and that with the tender love of a Father pitying His children, and knowing the frail clay and dust of which they are made? He sought us wandering in self-chosen paths, the paths of sin, He toiled after us as a shepherd wearying himself to find a lost sheep. Nor is He satisfied with seeking, but when He had found us, He took both us and our sorrows upon His own shoulders,—He was obedient unto the death on the Cross. Truly we may say that He loved us unto the death of the Cross, and the measure of His Love and His obedience is the same. When this love thoroughly fills a soul, it enjoys true peace of conscience; it is content and happy, asking neither greatness, nor fame, nor pleasures,—nothing, in short, which the lapse of time will sweep away and leave no trace behind. It seeks nothing save the Will of God, and it watches continually in blessed expectation of the Coming of the Bridegroom.

CXXXVI.

ON GRATITUDE.

FORGETFULNESS of self, of which we often hear as pertaining to those who seek after God in a generous spirit, does not interfere with gratitude for His Gifts. And for this reason: such forgetfulness does not lie in not being conscious of anything we possess, but rather in never confining ourselves to the contemplation of self, or dwelling upon our own good or evil in an exclusive or personal fashion. All such self-occupation severs us from pure and simple love, narrows the heart, and sets us further from true perfection by dint of seeking it in an excited, anxious, restless spirit, which comes of self-love.

But though we may forget ourselves, that is to say, we may not be studying self-interest alone, we shall not fail often to see ourselves truly. We shall not contemplate self out of egotism, but as we contemplate God there will often be a side light, so to say, thrown upon ourselves; just as a man who stands looking at the reflection of another in a large mirror, while looking for that other man he beholds himself, without seeking to do so. And thus we often see ourselves clearly, in the pure light of God. The Presence of God in purity and simplicity, sought after in very faithfulness, is like that large mirror, wherein we discern the tiniest spot that flecks our soul.

A peasant who has never passed beyond his own poor village realises its poverty but faintly. But set him amid splendid palaces and courts, and he will perceive how squalid his own home is, and how vile his rags compared with such magnificence. Even so we realise our own loathsomeness and unworthiness when brought face to face with the beauty and greatness of God.

Talk as much as you will of the vanity and emptiness

of the creature, the shortness and uncertainty of life, the inconstancy of fortune and friends, the delusions of grandeur, its inevitable and bitter disappointments, the failure of bright hopes, the void of all we attain, and the poignancy of the evils we endure; all these things, true and just as they are, do not touch the heart, they do not reach far, or alter a man's life. He sighs over the bondage of vanity, yet does not seek to break his bonds. But let one ray of heavenly light penetrate within, and forthwith beholding the depth of goodness, which is God, he likewise beholds the depth of evil, His fallen creature. Then he despises himself, hates, shuns, fears, renounces self; he throws himself upon God and is lost in Him. Thus it is that "one deep telleth another." Verily that man's loss is a blessed one, for he finds himself without seeking. He has no more selfish interests, but all turns to his profit, for everything turns to good for those who love God. He sees the mercies which issue forth from that abyss of weakness, sin, and nothingness; he sees and rejoices. And here observe that those who have not as yet made any great progress in self-renunciation still see all these mercies very much from the side which bears personal reference to themselves. For thorough setting aside of self-will is so rare in this life, that very few souls are able to look at the mercies they have received from anything but their own point of view; they rejoice in the All-powerful Hand which has saved them, so to say, in spite of themselves. But a really pure, wholly self-detached soul, such as are the Saints in Heaven, would feel the same joy and love over the mercies poured forth on others as on themselves; for, wholly forgetting self, they would love the Good Pleasure of God, the riches of His Grace, and His Glory, as set forth in the sanctification of others, as much as in their own. All would be the same, because " I " ceased to be: it would be no more " I " than another, but God Alone in all, to be loved, adored, and the sole joy of true, disinterested love. Such a soul is wrapt in wonder at His Mercies, not for its own sake, but for love of Him. It thanks Him that He has done His Will and glorified Himself, even as in the Lord's Prayer we ask Him that it may be done, and that His Kingdom may come. . . . But short of this blessed state, the soul is touched with gratitude for the benefits of which it is conscious; and as nothing is more dangerous than any attempt to soar beyond our vocation, so nothing is more harmful to the spiritual life than to lose sight of such sustenance as is suitable to its actual needs, by aiming at a higher standard of perfection than is fitted to us. When the soul feels deeply moved with gratitude for all God has done for it,- such gratitude should be cherished carefully, waiting till the time when God may see fit to purify it still more from all elements of self. The child who attempts to walk alone before its time is sure to fall; he must not tear off the leading-strings with which his nurse upholds him. Let us be content to live on gratitude, and be sure that though there may be a mingling of self-interest in it, it will strengthen our heart. Let us love God's Mercies, not merely for Himself and His Glory, but for ourselves and our eternal happiness; if eventually God should enlarge our hearts to contain a purer, more generous love, a love more unreservedly His, then we may safely and unhesitatingly yield to that more perfect love.

While, then, you adore God's Mercy, and are filled with wondering admiration at it; while you long above all things to fulfil His Will; while you marvel at the goodness with which He has made what seemed a "vessel of dishonour" to be unto honour,[1] pour out the most abundant thanksgiving of which you are capable; and remember that the purest of all God's Gifts is the power of loving them all for His Sake, not for your own.

CXXXVII.

TO ONE IN SPIRITUAL DISTRESS.

You see by God's Light in the depth of your conscience what grace requires of you; but you are resisting

[1] Rom. ix. 21.

God, and hence comes your trouble. You start by saying, "It is impossible that I can do what is required of me;" but this is a temptation of despair. Despair of yourself as much as you please, but not of God. He is both loving and powerful, and He will deal with you according to the measure of your faith. If you believe all you will attain all—you will move mountains; but if you believe nothing you will receive nothing, only it will be your own fault. Remember Abraham, who hoped against hope; and imitate the Blessed Virgin, who, when what seemed wholly impossible was set before her, answered unhesitatingly, "Be it unto me according to Thy Word."

So do not shut up your heart. It is not merely that you cannot do what is required of you, so straitened is your heart; but yet more, you do not want to be able to do it; you do not wish to have your heart enlarged; you are afraid lest it should be done. How can you expect grace to win entrance into a heart so resolutely closed to it? All that I would ask of you is to acquiesce calmly and in a spirit of faith, and not give ear to your own suggestions. Provided you will yield meekly, and gradually regain peace through recollection, everything will be achieved by degrees, and what in your present state of temptation seems impossible will become easy. Then we shall have you saying, "What, is this all!" Why so much despair and outcry for so simple a matter which God is bringing about and preparing so lovingly? Have a care lest in resisting Him you should estrange yourself from Him. All your religion would prove hollow if you should fail in this essential point,—all would lapse into mere indulgence of tastes and tendencies. I pray God that He will not suffer you so to fall away. I think much about your troubles, and I care far more for what involves a risk of resisting God than for the heaviest of other sorrows. Crosses borne with quiet endurance, lowliness, simplicity, and abnegation of self, unite us to Jesus Christ Crucified, and work untold good; but crosses which we reject through self-estimation and self-will separate us from Him, contract the heart, and by degrees dry up the fountains of grace. In God's Name I intreat you yield humbly, and without trusting to yourself, mere broken reed that you are, say, "To Him nothing is impossible." He only asks one "Yes," spoken in pure faith. Give me the comfort of hearing that you have uttered that "Yes" from the bottom of your heart. You will fill me with real joy amid my own sadness.

CXXXVIII.

THE LIFE OF PEACE.

Oct. 16, 1714.

I HAVE just returned from a long visitation tour and find your letter, to which I reply, 1*st*. Go on amid the shadows in evangelic simplicity, not stopping short either in feelings, or tastes, or the light of reason, or any unwonted gifts. Be content to believe, to obey, to die unto self, according to that state of life in which God has placed you.

2*nd*. You must not be discouraged by your involuntary distractions, which arise from your lively imagination and your active habits of business. Enough if you do not encourage such distractions in times of prayer by yielding overmuch to a voluntary dissipation of mind all through the day. People pour themselves out too much; they perform even good works with too much eagerness and excitement; they indulge their tastes and fancies, and then God punishes all this in their times of prayer. You must learn to act calmly and in continual dependence on the Spirit of Grace, which means mortification of all the hidden works of self-love.

3*rd*. Habitual intention, which is a reaching forth of the inmost soul to God, will suffice. This is to live in the Presence of God. Passing events would not find you thus minded, were it otherwise. Be still, and do not forfeit what you have at home by turning to seek abroad what you will not find. Never neglect out of mere carelessness to try and make your intentions more definite, but meanwhile your undefined, undeveloped intentions are good.

4*th*. A peaceful heart is a good sign, provided further that you heartily and lovingly obey God, and are watchful against self-love.

5*th*. Make use of your imperfections to learn self-detachment, and cleave to God only. Try to grow in all goodness, not that you may find a dangerous self-satisfaction therein, but that you may do the Will of your Beloved.

6*th*. Try to be simple, putting aside anxious retrospection, which self-love encourages under various pretexts: it will only disturb you and prove a snare. Those who lead a recollected, mortified, dependent life, through real desire to love God, will be quickly warned by that love whenever they sin against it; and directly you feel such warnings, pause. I repeat my injunction, be at rest. I daily pray before God's Holy Altar that He would keep you in His Own Unity and in the Grace of His Holy Spirit.

www.ingramcontent.com/pod-product-compliance
Lightning Source LLC
Chambersburg PA
CBHW030818230426
43667CB00008B/1268